Comprehensive Catalog and Encyclopedia of Morgan and Peace Dollars

PART III: THE PEACE SILVER DOLLAR

By
Leroy C. Van Allen
A. George Mallis

(With research and contributions in Chapter Five by Pete R. Bishal)

REVISED EDITION OF
Comprehensive Catlaogue and Encyclopedia of
U.S. Morgan and Peace Silver Dollars

Containing

POPULARITY OF COLLECTING & INVESTING
BACKGROUND OF SILVER DOLLAR COINAGE
CONDITION AVAILABILITY
DETAILS OF MINTING PROCESSES
HISTORICAL LETTERS ○ 2100+ ILLUSTRATIONS
DESCRIPTIONS OF 1800 ERRORS/VARIETIES
GSA SALE OF CARSON CITY DOLLARS
SILVER DOLLAR HOARDS
DETECTING COUNTERFEITS
PRESERVATION & STORAGE
GRADING

Published by

Rare Coin Investments (RCI)
P.O. Box C
Ironia, NJ 07845

Library of Congress Catalog Number: 2023904390

ISBN 979-8-9919648-0-7

Printed in the United States

THE HISTORY OF THE VAM BOOK

VAM book refers to the joint authorship book by Leroy Catlin Van Allen and A. George Mallis with a rather long title of *Comprehensive Catalog and Encyclopedia of Morgan and Peace Dollars*. The book had its genesis as independent efforts and books by both authors in the late 1950's and early 1960's. The following story briefly traces the development of these initial independent books and the later joint efforts to produce the various editions of the VAM book.

EARLY INDEPENDENT EFFORTS

In the mid-1950's, Mallis' collecting interests turned to Morgan dollars, since they were relatively inexpensive to collect and were in need of being catalogued. Beginning late 1958 as CEO of an architect firm, he made weekly trips to a job site at Bailey's Cross Roads in Alexandria, VA. Before returning home in Massachusetts, he would purchase a thousand dollar bag of silver dollars from the Treasury Department sales counter in Washington DC. Each bag was subsequently checked and recorded for dates, mint marks, and varieties. When the Treasury Department stopped issuing silver dollars in 1964, Mallis had examined some THIRTY-FIVE THOUSAND of them. When the Treasury released the scarce New Orleans Morgan dollars late in 1962, Van Allen became interested in them. From early 1963 through 1964, he examined some ten-thousand silver dollars from the Treasury Department in Washington, DC and the Baltimore Federal Reserve.

Mallis began preparing a pamphlet in 1962 of his recordings on the silver dollars he had examined. In mid-1963, Francis Kleas published a pamphlet entitled *Die Varieties of Morgan Silver Dollars*. This was a real eye opener with large clear photos of some major varieties. It was Klaes' pamphlet that started Van Allen writing an independent manuscript on Morgan varieties in late 1963. He thought Klaes' listings and photographs could be expanded with additional varieties.

Van Allen's first manuscript was sent to Neil Shafer of Whitman Publishing early in 1964. Shafer advised him that it was NOT READY for publication and that he needed to consult the mint records to explain the WHY of the varieties (as he had in several articles). Van Allen then spent a good deal of the spring of 1964 at the National Archives and Library of Congress in Washington, DC gathering material and studying additional coins.

In the spring of 1964, Mallis approached Klaes about collaborating on a revised list of Morgan dollar die varieties, but this partnership never developed. Mallis then continued his research alone. In October 1964, this effort was completed with his distribution of 50 free copies of a pamphlet entitled *List of Die Varieties of Morgan*

Head Silver Dollars. The pamphlets were distributed to interested numismatists and libraries.

By September 1964, Van Allen sent a completely revised manuscript of the Morgan dollar series varieties to Charles "Shotgun" Slade III (a prominent silver dollar dealer who owned a printing shop). Slade thought the manuscript was of interest but that a SHORTER pamphlet would be more suitable for him to publish. In October 1964, Van Allen submitted a new manuscript on the 1878 Morgan varieties to Slade. He then suggested a DIE CLASSIFICATION SYSTEM was needed and that Sheldon's *Penny Whimsy* should be studied. Taking his suggestion, Van Allen rewrote the 1878 dollar manuscript and resubmitted it to him late in November 1964. This book was not printed as scheduled in February 1965 and the manuscript was again revised and forwarded to Slade in March 1965.

After some negotiations in early 1965, Walter Breen agreed to act as consulting or collaborating author with Mallis on a new book, *United States Silver Dollars, Morgan Type.* Unfortunately, Breen suffered a lengthy illness and was unable to assist in the manuscript preparation. Mallis pressed on alone and copyrighted the complete manuscript in June 1965. He worked with Whitman Publishing in 1965 to prepare the book for publication, but the project was abandoned early in 1966 because of the efforts with Van Allen. Only THREE copies of this manuscript exist - one in the Library of Congress, one with Mallis and one with Van Allen (extensively marked up as a basis for the later collaboration effort).

At this point, Van Allen decided to publish his own book entitled *Morgan and Peace Dollar Varieties.* His wife, Ruth, typed the camera ready copy and 5,000 softbound and 100 hardbound copies were printed by December 1965. Izzy Fishman of Ace Coin Exchange in Baltimore, Maryland distributed the books which were sold out within about a year at a retail price of $2.50.

VAN ALLEN AND MALLIS JOINT EFFORTS

In January 1966, Mallis suggested to Van Allen that their two works and Shafer's efforts should be combined into ONE reference work. Mallis and Van Allen first met at Mallis' home in Massachusetts in April 1966 to discuss a joint book venture. Jim Johnson of Coin World's Collectors' Clearinghouse was very much in favor of such a project and endorsed it several times in Coin World in 1965. Walter Breen had also recommended the collaboration in his November 1964 column in Coin world.

In June 1966, Whitman Publishing was contacted concerning the publication of their joint book on silver dollar varieties. Whitman Publishing would not accept the project since it was not one hundred percent ready with each variety of silver dollar verified. The manuscript was completely ready in mid 1986. Then began a long string of publisher rejection notices! Twelve publishers declined offers to print the book.

Meanwhile, new varieties of silver dollars were pointed out to the authors by various coin collectors. This kept increasing the size of the manuscript.

In February 1971, the authors decided to finance the publication of the book and Van Allen's wife, Ruth, again typed the final text. Van Allen pasted the camera ready copy. By December 1971, 2,610 softbound and 205 hardbound copies were received from the printer with the title of *Guide to Morgan and Peace Dollars*. Frank and Louise Katen of Katen Coins in Silver Springs Maryland distributed the book. These books were sold in about a year and a half. By 1975, the book had become hard to find and the going price for a copy was two to three times its original price.

Collectors continued to point out new varieties to the authors. By mid 1975, enough new material had accumulated that it was time to revise the VAM book as it had become known. A publishing agreement was made with First Coinnvestors of Long Island, New York and Arco Publishing delivered 5,500 hardbound books in October 1976 followed by 2,800 hardbound and 50 leather bound books were delivered in December 1976. Minor changes were incorporated in the second printing of 4,500 hardbound books delivered in March 1977. The retail price of the initial printing of the book was $19.95 and the title was *Comprehensive Catalogue and Encyclopedia of U.S. Morgan and Peace Silver Dollars*. This second edition had four printings with the last one in 1981. There were more than 20,000 hardbound copies printed. In 1977, it received the Book of the Year award from the Numismatic Literary Guild.

A great many new varieties were reported by collectors after the 1976 book release and new material on silver dollars accumulated during the coin market boom of the late 1970's and early 1980's. The authors intended to publish a revised edition of the VAM book in the mid 1980's and the manuscript was ready by early 1986. Meanwhile, Arco Publishing had been sold and was no longer interested in publishing the book and First Coinvestors had moved and lost most of the negatives. The book had to be typeset again and Van Allen had to reprint the majority of the book photos from his old film negatives.

From 1986 through 1991, the authors were unable to find a publisher for the VAM book. In 1991, DLRC Press of Virginia Beach, Virginia agreed to republish the book. Further additions and revisions were made and the third edition was released in September 1992 at $49.95 retail with 4,400 softbound and 600 hardbound copies printed. The VAM book again received the Book of the Year award from the Numismatic Literary Guild in 1993, and had the title of *Comprehensive Catalog and Encyclopedia of Morgan and Peace Dollars*.

Leroy Van Allen

Glossary of Abbreviations

MINT MARKS:

P	Philadelphia
O	New Orleans
S	San Francisco
CC	Carson City
D	Denver

OTHERS:

Obv.	Obverse
Rev.	Reverse
TF	Tail Feathers
PAF	Parallel Arrow Feathers
SAF	Slanted Arrow Feathers
I...IV	Type of Mint Mark or Obverse Design
A...D	Type of Reverse Design
O/O	O Repunched Over O
O/S	O Repunched Over S
O/CC	O Repunched Over CC
II/I Obv.	Second Design Obverse Over First Design Obverse
7/8TF	Seven Over Eight Tail Feathers
BU	Brilliant Uncirculated

RARITY SCALE:

R-1	Common (Tens of Millions)
R-2	Not so Common (Several Millions)
R-3	Scarce (Hundreds of Thousands)
R-4	Very Scarce (Tens of Thousands)
R-5	Rare (Several Thousands)
R-6	Very Rare (Several Hundred)
R-7	Extremely Rare (Few Tens)
R-8	Unique or Nearly Unique (Several)

INTEREST FACTOR:

I-1 Normal die variety with little interest to variety collectors .

I-2 Minor die variety with some interest to variety collectors.

I-3 Significant die variety with general interest to variety collectors.

I-4 Major die variety with universal interest to variety collectors.

I-5 Outstanding die variety with prime interest to variety collectors.

AMPLIFYING DESCRIPTIONS:

I-1 Normal die variety with no unusual die states. Can have hairline die cracks, small die chips, or minor clash marks which are normal as die wears or portions of the design may be weak due to polishing of the die.

I-2 Minor variations from normal die such as slight shifts in date or mint mark placement and orientation; micro doubling of date or mint mark; and slight abnormalities in die state such as fairly large die cracks or die chips (i.e., spiked dates). Such die variations may not be of interest to all collectors but they are identifiable using a medium power magnifying glass.

I-3 Significant variations from normal die such as changes in mint mark or date digit sizes; small die design changes; large shifts in date or mint mark placement and orientation; major doubling of date or mint mark; slight doubling of die design; small modifications of individual dies (touch ups, polishing, and weak overdates and over mint marks), and large abnormalities in die state such as big die cracks or gouges. These die variations are of general interest to many variety collectors and are usually noticeable with a low power magnifying glass.

I-4 Major variations from normal die such as large die design changes; unusually large doubling of date or mint mark; large doubled die design; and strong individual die modifications of date or mint mark (i.e., over dates and over mint marks). Most of these die variations are visible to the naked eye and are of universal interest to variety collectors.

I-5 An outstanding major die variation representing the best example of its type.

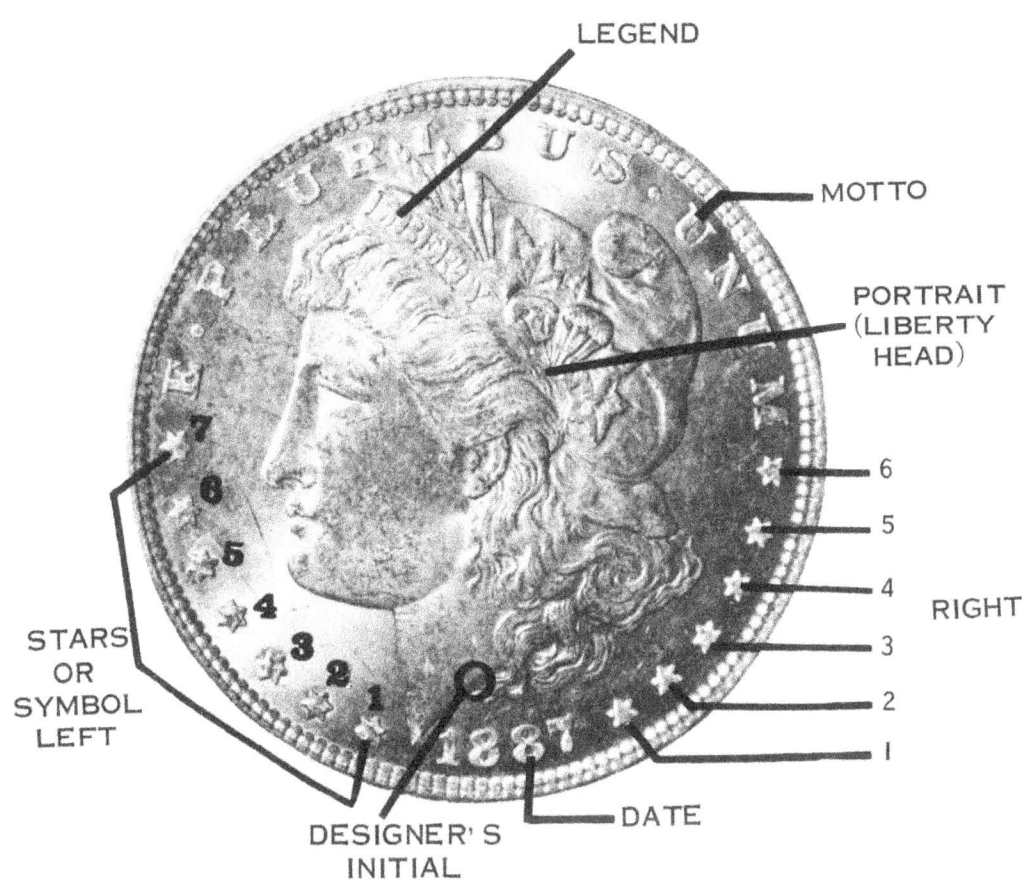

LEGEND

MOTTO

PORTRAIT
(LIBERTY
HEAD)

6

5

4

RIGHT

3

2

I

STARS
OR
SYMBOL
LEFT

7

6

5

4

3

2

1

1887

DESIGNER'S
INITIAL

DATE

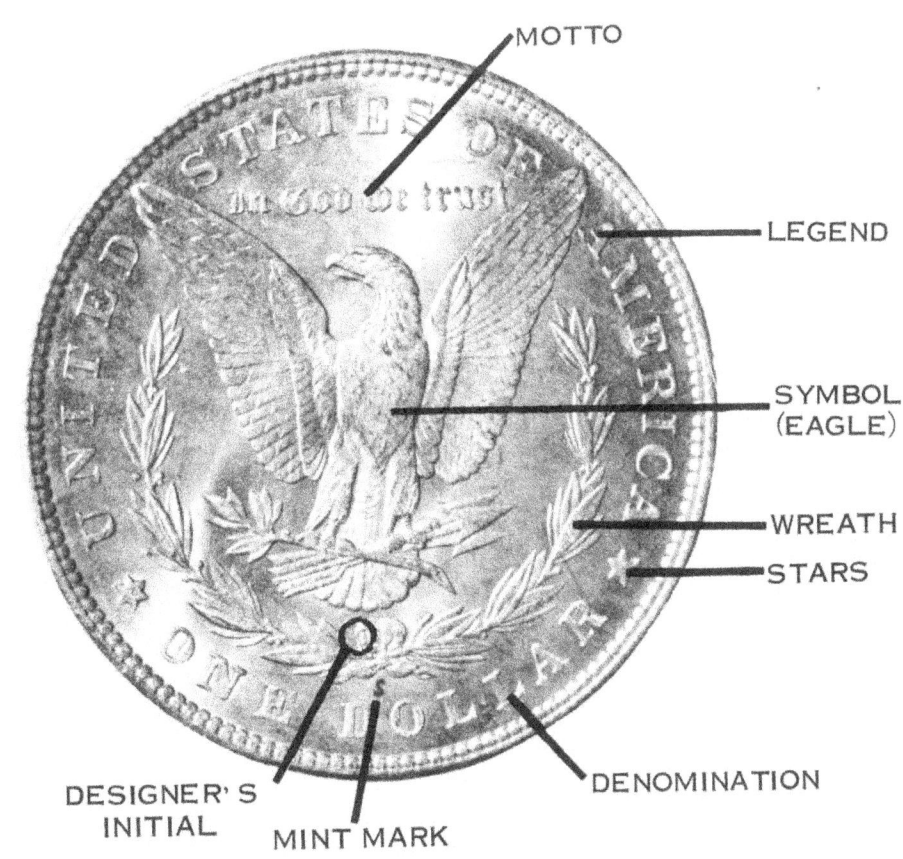

MOTTO

In God we trust

LEGEND

SYMBOL
(EAGLE)

WREATH

STARS

DESIGNER'S
INITIAL

MINT MARK

DENOMINATION

Part III

Table of Contents

Part III
The Peace Silver Dollar

The minting of the Peace silver dollar was first suggested by Farren Zerbe of San Francisco, California, a veteran numismatist and the official historian of the American Numismatic Association (ANA), at the Chicago ANA Convention in August, 1920. Zerbe presented a paper at this convention entitled, "Commemorate the Peace with a Coin for Circulation," which proposed that a new coin be issued by the U. S. Government commemorating the signing of the peace treaty between the United States and Germany at the end of World War I. The paper stated that "our Peace coin should be of good size for art effects, and if it be one for popular use by all the people, the half dollar...would be a common choice. But should we resume the coinage of the silver dollar, that coin should be a consideration."[1]

The ANA recommended that the dollar be a commemorative coin and be issued for general circulation. However, it was pointed out that the commemorative coins had never been issued for general circulation, but were usually sold at a premium to raise funds for expositions or memorial projects, which prevented them from reaching general circulation.[2]

The ANA appointed a five-member committee under the chairmanship of Judson Brenner of Youngstown, Ohio, to propose the bill to Congress. Members of the committee, besides Zerbe, were Dr. J. M. Henderson of Columbus, Ohio; Congressman William A. Ashbrook of Jamestown, Ohio; and Howland Wood of New York City. During December 1920, the committee met with Congressman Albert H. Vestal, Chairman of the House Committee on Coinage, Weights and Measures. As a result, a joint resolution was presented to Congress on May 9, 1921, proposing that a coin be struck commemorating the end of the war.[3] This was the same day that coinage of the Morgan silver dollar was resumed. This joint resolution stated:[4]

To Provide for the Coinage of Peace Dollars

RESOLVED by the Senate and House of Representatives of the United States of America in Congress assembled, That as soon as practicable after the passage of this resolution, all standard silver dollars coined under the provisions of Section 2 of the Act entitled 'An Act to conserve the gold supply of the United States; to provide silver for subsidiary coinages and for commercial use; to assist foreign Governments at war with the enemies of the United States; and for the above purposes to stabilize the price and encourage the production of silver,' approved April 23, 1918 [Pittman Act], shall be of an appropriate design commemorative of the terminations of the war between the Imperial German Government and the people of the United States.

Such design shall be selected by the Director of the Mint with the approval of the Secretary of the Treasury. Each standard silver dollar of such design shall be known as the 'Peace Dollar.'

The joint resolution encountered no difficulties until Congressman Vestal asked permission to have it placed on the unanimous consent calendar, which would have assured its passage. A member of the House objected to this procedure, and the resolution was placed on the regular calendar. Later debate on the resolution showed that the Congressmen were reluctant to recommend a silver dollar coinage. Congress eventually adjourned without voting on the resolution.[5]

Later the coin was authorized without Congressional action, under the provisions of the Pittman Act of April 23, 1918. The Secretary of the Treasury, Andrew W. Mellon, gave approval to change the design of the silver dollar. The Morgan design had existed for 43 years; and the 1890 Act only prevented design changes more often than every 25 years.

Under an executive order by President Harding on July 28, 1921, all essential matters relating to the design of medals, insignia, and coins produced by the executive departments were to be submitted, for advice on the merit of such designs, to the executive officer of the Commission of Fine Arts.[6]

INITIAL DESIGN

The Commission of Fine Arts held a contest for the design. Invitations to eight leading sculptors of the U.S. to submit designs for the new standard dollar were sent on November 23, 1921. Those submitting sketches

Farran Zerbe

1921
Peace Dollar

were: Robert Aitken, Chester Beach, Victor D. Brenner, Anthony De Francisci, John Flanagan, Henry Hering, Hermon A. MacNeil, and Adolf Weinman. The winner was to receive a prize of $1,500 upon completion of a finished model and the others were to receive $100 each. The eventual winner, De Francisci of New York City, submitted two sets of sketches on December 13, 1921. He had two ideas and wanted to present them both.

Anthony De Francisci came from Italy and served under Weinman and was also an apprentice to James E. Fraser, designer of the Indian Head - Buffalo nickel and Herman MacNeil, designer of the Standing Liberty quarter. He only had three weeks to submit his sketches and was 33 at that time. In developing the design of the Liberty Head, he utilized his new bride of 22, Teresa Cafarelli (also from Italy), as a model in their Manhattan studio. He stated that "I was unable, owing to the shortness of time, to engage in the search of a model akin to my mind's picture – that is, a professional model. I do derive some help from the features of Mrs. De Francisci, but generally the Liberty head as it stands is a composite one.[7] De Francisci described how he used Teresa as a model.[8] "I opened the window of my studio and let the wind blow on her hair while she was posing for me... The nose, the fullness of the eye and the mouth are much like my wife's, although the whole face has been elongated." He went on to say in remarks reported on January 12, 1922 by the Minneapolis Tribune.[9] "You will see that the Liberty is not a photograph of Mrs. De Francisci. It is a composite face and in that way typifies something of America. I did not try to execute an 'American type' or a picture of any woman. I wanted the Liberty to express something of the spirit of the country – the intellectual speed and vigor and vitality America has, as well as

Teresa De Francisci

its youth..."

Each of the two reverse designs originally submitted by De Francisci showed an eagle with a broken sword to symbolize disarmament. One showed the eagle standing on the sword, literally breaking it with its beak. The second showed the eagle clutching a broken sword with olive branches over its head. James E. Fraser, a sculptor member of the Commission of Fine Arts, and De Francisci visited the Director of the Mint in Washington, D. C. on December 15 and again on December 19 to make some alterations in the models and in connection with their submission for approval to the Secretary of the Treasury. The initial reverse approved on December 19 showed the eagle clutching a broken sword.

Reaction to the description of this approved design as published on December 19 was critical of the broken sword, however, as related by O'Reilly of the Bureau of the Mint:[10]

> The accepted model for the reverse of the standard dollar bears at its base of the eagle a device representing a broken sword. As a result of published description of the model numerous protests against use of this device are being received.
>
> Mr. Fraser, the sculptor member of the Fine Arts Commission has suggested in a telegram received this morning that the broken sword be removed from the model.
>
> Mr. Charles Moore, Chairman of the F.A.C. has also suggested that the broken be not used as part of the design.

As a result of these protests an olive branch was substituted for the broken sword and the revised models were submitted to the Secretary of the Treasury on December 23 for his approval.[11] Mr. De Francisci visited the Philadelphia Mint on December 21, 22, 23, and 28 for consultation in changes in the reverse model design and master hub preparation.[12]

The modified design was approved on December 24 and the dies were ready for coinage on December 29, 1921, just a scant three days from years end, as related by acting Mint Director O'Reilly:[13]

The Sec., Under Sec., Moore, Fraser all approve design without sword. Your telegram today completes authority. Francisci at Phil today to supervise preparation of hub. Dies will be ready for coinage 29th. Under Sec. does not wish to give publicity to change hence issued newspaper notice your name stating sword which appeared upon one of the models submitted does not appear on coin. Very widespread protest against use of broken sword...

From December 29 to 31, 1921, a total of 1,006,473 pieces in high relief were struck. At least five matte proofs and perhaps two dozen or so satin proofs were struck at this time. The first specimen of the Peace silver dollar went by special messenger on January 3, 1922 to President Harding; others were delivered to the Secretary of the Treasury and to the Director the Mint, Washington, D.C.[14] The new dollars were released into general circulation on the same day.

The obverse of the coin shows a classic Liberty Head with a tiara of rays of light above her head. The word LIBERTY appears around the top of the head and IN GOD WE TRUST is inscribed at either side of the neck. The date is at the bottom.

On the reverse, a bald eagle is shown perched on a mountain crag with rays emanating from the lower right of the coin. Although the sun does not show, the rays shine as a token of the dawn of a new era, symbolic of the abolishment of war and the perpetuation of peace. The eagle holds an olive branch in its talons. In a semicircle at the top of the coin are the inscriptions UNITED STATES OF AMERICA, and below this, E PLURIBUS UNUM. In the lower half appear the words ONE DOLLAR, with PEACE at the very bottom of the coin.

Reaction to the new silver dollars was mixed. The Liberty head was criticized as having a startled or unkempt look. *The Wall Street Journal* had an article entitled "Our Flapper Silver Dollar."[15] There was also talk that the high relief of the design prevented the coins from stacking well. But perhaps their greatest shortcoming was the weak, flat strikes with central details of the coin not being brought out – particularly the central hairlines of the Liberty Head.

At that time, George T. Morgan was the Chief Engraver of the Mint. Thus, there was again a similar set of circumstances reminiscent of the problems encountered in 1878 on the Morgan silver dollar when Morgan was a special engraver. He was under time pressure to perfect the Morgan silver dollar dies in 1878 – the main problem being too high relief causing the dies to break and to wear out rapidly. Forty three years later, Morgan was again under time pressure to produce a new silver dollar design. The final design models were not approved until December 23, 1921, which left only a week to pre-

pare the working dies and to strike coins before the end of the year. As a result, the dies produced were not completely satisfactory for striking production coins - the problem being too high relief.

DESIGN CHANGES IN OF THE REGULAR COINAGE

George Morgan wrote De Francisci early in January 1922 about changing the design relief of the new Peace dollar. He stated:[16]

I know you will be disappointed but the pressure necessary to bring up the work was so destructive to the dies that we got tired of putting new dies in.

A January 10, 1922 letter from the Acting Director of the Mint, O'Reilly to the Superintendent of the Philadelphia Mint reiterated the difficulties with the high relief 1921 design:

Request you to discontinue all work on preparation of dies for 1922 silver dollars.

It is understood from your letter of Jan. 6, 1922, that the relief of model from which dies were prepared for 21 coins is too great, and its distribution and areas not wisely planned; that the highest relief on each side is in the center of the coin and to attempt to drive the metal into this part of the coin brings a fin to the outer edge and breaks the die, and that this results in a decided difference in thickness which mars the appearance of the coin and interferes with stacking. It is also understood that the change is necessary to bring the model nearer to coin relief, and that such changes could be made at the mint without changing design, after consulting with its designer.

In accordance with your suggestion over the telephone it has been decided to take the matter up with the FAC with a view to procuring from Mr. Francisci a new model of lower relief. In doing this it is understood no change will be made in the design of the coin...

The same day O'Reilly sent a letter to the Director of the Mint, Baker, who was out West at the time:[17]

Experiments with 1922 dies like those sent Denver and San Francisco show relief still too high. Absolutely necessary have new model made by Francisci lowering relief to get coin to stack. No change whatever in design. Have today wired Denver and S.F. not to start dollar coinage until further instructed. Taking up matter with F.A.C. tomorrow.

This letter indicates that high relief coins with 1922 date were struck at Philadelphia Mint early in January in 1922, but were undoubtedly destroyed since they were experimental. High relief dies had been sent to the Denver Mint on January 6 but were returned on January 12.[18]

In mid-January 1922, Morgan slightly modified the design by adding two short rays in front on the obverse, and strengthened the letters, the details of hair, the feathers, and the mountain. At least five trial pieces were struck in matte proof of these slightly modified but still high relief 1922 dollars.[19]

Confirming telephone communications requesting that trial pieces, about 5 in number, struck from dies of new dollars now being prepared, be sent to Mr. Jones E. Fraser, Sculptor member of F.A.C. for inspection and report. I have also to request that at lease 2 pieces be sent from the same experimental strike to Director of Mint. It is understood that these trial pieces are to be returned to you by Mr. Fraser, and by this Bureau.

Apparently the Bureau of the Mint did not destroy these trial pieces as Breen reports five pieces known of the high relief 1922 Peace dollar.[20] Since their design differed from subsequent 1922 coins, these trial pieces in matte proof are among the rarest of silver dollar types.

This high relief 1922 design was still not satisfactory for striking regular coins. So later in January 1922, De Francisci was called to the Philadelphia Mint to supervise the production of the new master die by the Janvier engraving machine.[21] The relief of the design was made lower which De Francisci was understandably unhappy about but which he also realized had to be done. Further changes to the design detail were made without the knowledge or consent of De Francisci by George Morgan.[22] Concave fields were made flat, and small changes were made in the olive branches, rays, hairlines, feathers, and mountains.

Several proof satin finish dollars of the lower relief design were struck.[23, 24] Regular business strikes were produced by all three mints, Philadelphia, Denver, and San Francisco. But these initial 1922 low relief dies were still not completely satisfactory. Many of these early low relief design coins show a weakness in strike in the hair over the ear and on the eagle's wing feathers above the leg. This initial 1922 low relief design shows a detached olive branch from the eagle's foot and two hills to the right of the mountain crag. Only one or two dies of this initial low relief design was used at the Philadelphia Mint making them fairly scarce for that large issue of coins. About one-third of the 1922 Denver Mint coins and about one-half of the 1922 San Francisco Mint coins were of this design. It is well known that 1922-S coins are typically weakly struck.

Some minor design changes to the reverse were made shortly after the introduction of the lower relief design in 1922. The olive branch was made to go up against the eagle's right foot, a third hill was added to the right of the other two, the talon was connected to the toe of the eagle's left claw, and the rays around DOLLAR were strengthened. The obverse design was not changed. The field radius of the master obverse and reverse dies were probably changed to allow fuller striking of the design.

The low relief design was used for the remaining years of the Peace dollar series. Only a couple of very minor changes to the obverse design was made when the coinage resumed in 1935. The 1935-S was also struck with a design showing an added fourth ray below ONE and a seventh ray added below the eagle's tail. This was apparently a left over experimental die made during 1922.[25]

Footnotes

[1] Walter Breen, "The 1922 Type of 1921 Peace Dollar," *The Numismatic Scrapbook Magazine*, July 1961, p. 1723.

[2] "New U. S. Silver Dollar to Employ Controversial Peace Coin Design," *Coin World*, August 19, 1964, p. 3.

[3] Ibid.

[4] Breen, p. 1724.

[5] Ibid.

[6] *Coin World*, August 19, 1964, p. 3.

[7] Ibid.

[8] Don Taxay, *The U.S. Mint and Coinage*, 1966, Arco Publishing.

[9] Ibid.

[10] Memo for Under Secretary by O'Reilly, Bureau of the Mint, December 23, 1921.

[11] Letter from Raymond T. Baker, Director of the Mint, to Secretary of the Treasury, December 23, 1921.

[12] Letter from Baker to Superintendent U.S. Mint Philadelphia, January 28, 1922.

[13] Telegram from Acting Dir. of Mint to Baker, c/o U. S. Mint San Francisco, December 24, 1921.

[14] Breen, p. 1725.

[15] Joseph Moss, "Peace Dollar," *The Numismatist*, July, 1942.

[16] Ed Reiter, "The Lady on the Dollar," *COINage*, 1978.

[17] Letter from O'Reilly to Baker c/o Checkline Banking & Trust Co., Reno, Nevada, January 10, 1922.

[18] Letter from Baker to Superintendent U.S. Mint Denver, February 27, 1922.

[19] Letter O'Reilly to Superintendent U.S. Mint Philadelphia, January 14, 1922.

[20] Walter Breen, *Encyclopedia of U.S. and Colonial Proof Coins: 1722–1977*, F.C.I. Press, Inc., New York 1977, p. 220.

[21] Breen, "The 1922 Type of 1921 Peace Dollar," p. 1726.

[22] Ibid

[23] Walter Breen, *Encyclopedia of U.S. and Colonial Proof Coins: 1722–1977*, 1977 F.C.I. Press, p. 221.

[24] Wayne, Miller, *The Morgan and Peace Dollar Textbook*, Adam Smith Publishing, 1983.

[25] T.W. Voetter, *The Numismatist*, October, 1940.

Chapter 12

Description of the Designs

The Peace silver dollar had several design changes, three for the obverse and four for the reverse. The first changes of the design were made in 1922 to correct some of the difficulties experienced with the high relief 1921 design. This high relief caused the dies to wear rapidly, the full design could not always be brought out (particularly the hairlines on the obverse), and the coins did not stack well. Further changes were made in 1934 and 1935 after a lapse from the 1928 of silver dollar coinage. A list of differences with accompanying photographs of the designs are included at the end of this chapter.

REVERSE DESIGN DESCRIPTIONS

The initial reverse design, A, was used on all coins struck at the Philadelphia Mint late in 1921 and for a few proof coins. The major characteristic of this design was the very high relief.

The second reverse design, B, was used on all 1922 to 1928, 1934, 1935-P, and some 1935-S coins. The relief of the design was considerably reduced, minor changes were made on the eagle, and the number of light rays was reduced. There are two versions of this B reverse. The first, B^1, has a detached olive branch from the eagle's foot, only two hills to the right of the mountain crag, a detached talon from the toe at the rear of the eagle's left claw, and weakness in some of the rays where they meet the tops of D–AR. This was discovered by Robert Maxey of Baltimore, MD and reported by Herbert P. Hicks in the January and February 1981 issues of the *Error–Variety News*. The B^1 reverse appears on a few of the 1922-P, about one third of the 1922-D and about one half of the 1922-S.

Since the B^1 reverse tended to result in weakly struck coins, it was modified early in 1922 to a B^2 reverse. The field curvature was changed to provide more fully struck coins and a number of minor design improvements and corrections were made. The olive branch was extended to meet the eagle's foot, a third hill was added to the right of the other two and some lines were added to strengthen their detail, the tail of R in DOLLAR was made slightly longer and extends past the vertical ray, the talon was attached to the toe at the rear of the eagle's left claw, and the rays intersect the DOLLAR letters in full relief.

The third reverse design C, was used on only a few 1935-S coins. Thus, we have the unusual situation that a design change was made for, or at, only one branch mint!. This reverse is the same as the previous reverse except for two small additions: a fourth ray was added below ONE, and a seventh ray was added below the eagle's tail.

These added rays are in approximately the same position as the extra rays used in the 1921 reverse. This variety was discovered by Mr. Berghli of San Diego, California, and was reported by T.W. Voetter in the May 1939, *The Numismatist.*

A possible explanation of the cause of this die variety was given by Voetter in a later article in the October 1940, issue of *The Numismatist.* In 1922 two different reverse hubs may have been made but one of them was unsatisfactory and was destroyed after making only a few working dies. One of these dies was later sent to the San Francisco Mint and was not used for coinage until 1935.

Since the coins struck at the Philadelphia Mint in 1935 were all of the second reverse type, this extra rays reverse design was only used at the San Francisco Mint. Only about one fourth to one third of the 1935-S coins have the added rays, which indicates that only one of the dies used had these extra rays (about 2 million 1935-S dollars were struck, and one Peace dollar die could strike up to half a million dollars before being retired).

OBVERSE DESIGN DESCRIPTIONS

The first obverse design, I, was also used on all coins struck at the Philadelphia Mint late in 1921 and for a few 1922 proof coins. It, too, had a very high relief as well as a slightly concave field.

The second obverse design, II, was used during 1922 to 1928. The relief was greatly reduced and the field was made much flatter. Changes in design detail included thinner letters and numbers, three additional short rays at the front of the cap, and a second line in the head band.

When the minting of the Peace dollar was resumed in 1934, slight obverse design changes were again made. In the third obverse design, III, the motto lettering was made thinner and the tail of the R in TRUST was straightened. Why the motto lettering was changed is a mystery, since the Liberty head design was not changed. Perhaps a new master die was made using the original Galvano with the basic design and the motto was added separately. However, the dies and hubs used in 1928 should have still been available in 1934; they obviously were available for the reverse, since it was not changed in 1934.

DESIGN COMBINATIONS

Table 12-1 shows the design combinations for the Peace silver dollar. Although three different designs are known for both the obverse and reverse, only four separate combinations exist.

I Obverse. Used in 1921 only. Differs from later design in following ways:

   a. Higher relief and concave field.
   b. Letters and numbers thicker.
   c. Rays from cap thicker, first three short rays missing on left.
   d. Only one line in head band.

A Reverse. Used in 1921 only. Differs from the later design in following ways:

   a. Higher relief.
   b. Less curved eagle's beak.
   c. Earlier division of branch at eagle's feet and different shaped leaves.
   d. Eagle's right ankle thinner.
   e. Eagle's left ankle showing.
   f. Mountain ranges different; only two peaks show instead of three.
   g. Four rays below ONE instead of three.
   h. Eight rays below eagle's tail instead of six.
   i. Twenty-one rays below eagle's wing instead of nineteen and one half, some rays shorter.

II Obverse. Used During 1922 to 1928.

B Reverse. Used for all 1922 to 1928, 1934, 1935-P, and some 1935-S.

Table 12-1 DESIGN COMBINATIONS FOR PEACE DOLLAR

Obverse	Mint	Reverse
I	all 1921 & some 1922 proofs	A
II	some 1922-P,D,S and some 1922 proofs	B¹
II	some 1922-P,D,S; all 1923 to 1928	B²
III	all 1934, 1935-P, and some 1935-S	B²
III	some 1935-S	C

MINOR DESIGN TYPES:

B¹ Reverse. Detached olive branch from eagle's foot, two hills to right of mountain crag, detached talon from toe at rear of eagle's left claw, R in DOLLAR is short, and rays are weak where they meet the tops of D–AR.

B² Reverse. Olive branch connected to eagle's foot, third hill added to right of mountain crag, talon connected to toe at rear of eagle's left claw, R in DOLLAR is slightly longer and extends past the vertical ray, and rays intersect DOLLAR letters in full relief.

B¹ Reverse. Detached olive branch

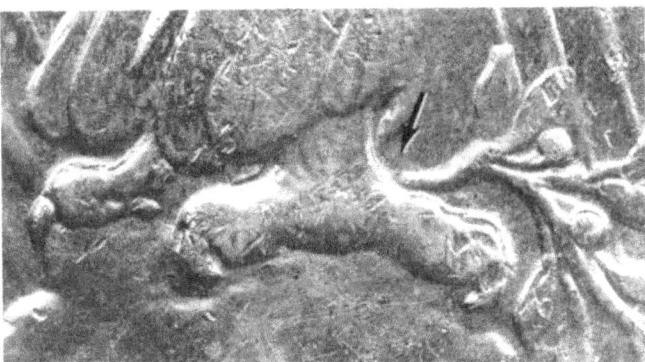

B² Reverse. Connected olive branch

B¹ Reverse. Two hills

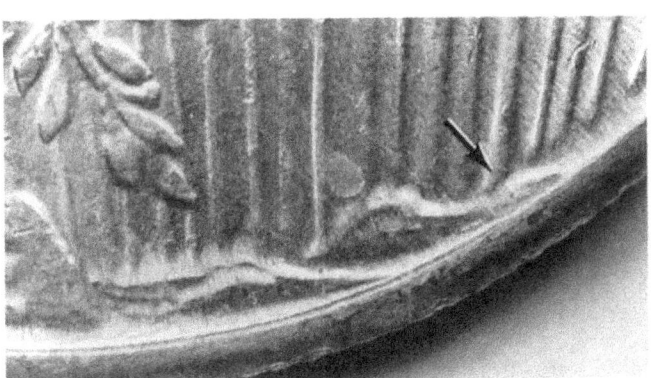

B² Reverse. Three Hills

III Obverse. Used in 1934 and 1935. Differs from earlier design in following ways:
    a. IN GOD WE TRUST lettering thinner.
    b. Straight tail on R in TRUST.

C Reverse. Used for some 1935-S. Differs from earlier design in following ways:
    a. Added fourth ray below ONE.
    b. Added seventh ray below eagle's tail.

Chapter 13

Discussion of Significant Varieties

MINT MARK VARIATIONS

Two branch mints struck the Peace silver dollar. The San Francisco Mint struck them from 1922 to 1928 and again in 1934 and 1935. Only one size mint mark was used – a micro S. The Denver Mint struck Peace dollars in 1922, 1923, 1926, 1927, and 1934. A micro D was used in all these years; in addition, a medium size D was used on some 1934 coins. The following is a list and description of various mint marks used:

San Francisco:

I S   Micro S: 1922–1928, 1934, and 1935

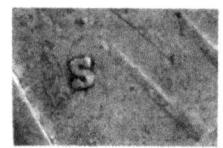

Denver:

I D   Micro D: 1922, 1923, 1926, 1927
                                    and some 1934

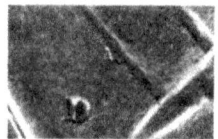

II D   Medium D: some 1934

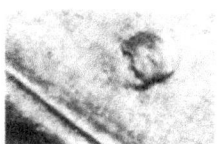

MINT MARK PLACEMENT

Only a few die variations are known of the mint mark placement for the Peace dollar series. The following is the short list of this variety. The 1935-S listed is of the type B reverse.

1926-D	D tilted right	1934-D	High D
1926-S	Medium high S	1934-D	D tilted right
1926-S	High S	1934-S	S tilted left
1927-S	High S	1935-S	S tilted left
1928-S	Medium high S		

DATE VARIATIONS

There were small differences in the numbers used for the date each year. Five different 1's were used and four different 2's. The fact that there were so many different design 1's and 2's on the Peace silver dollar indicates that the complete date was changed for almost every year on the master die using a logotype.

I 1	Thick 1	1921	
II 1	Rounded top 1	1922, 1925 – 1928	
III 1	Pointed top 1	1923	
IV 1	Tall large top 1	1924	
V 1	Small top 1	1934, 1935	
I 2	Thick 2	1921	
II 2	Straight bottom 2, rounded end	1922, 1924, 1926-1928	
III 2	Large end 2	1923	
IV 2	End of 2 slanting upwards	1925	
I 3	Small closed 3	1923	
II 3	Large open 3	1934, 1935	
I 4	Small 4	1924	

II 4	Large 4	1934 
I 5	Small 5	1925 
II 5	Large 5	1935 
I 6		1926 
I 7		1927 
I 8		1928 
I 9	Wide 9	1921 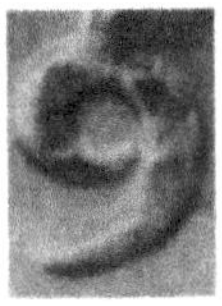
II 9	Thin 9, circular opening	1922–1928 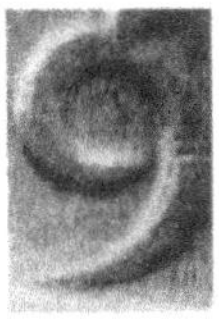
III 9	Thin 9, oblong opening	1934, 1935 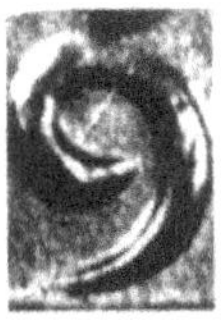

CLASHED DIES

As in the case of the Morgan silver dollars, clashed dies were common with the Peace silver dollars. The clashed reverse shows as an extra line extending up from the top of the eagle's right wing (an impression from the back of Liberty's neck), a vee above the eagle's left wing (from the junction of the neck and chin of the Liberty head), a raised bump or short curved vertical line above LL in DOLLAR (from the end of the headband), and a horizontal line extending from the branches below DOLLAR (from the top of the Liberty head below the R.

The clashed obverse shows as an extra line extending down from the chin and neck junction to the top of the E in WE (an impression of the second ray from the top of the left wing – in this case the obverse line is incused rather than raised, since it is incused in the reverse die), an incused vertical line at the end of the

head band (from the rays above DOLLAR on the reverse), and a short vertical line between the rays to the right of E in LIBERTY (from the branches on the reverse).

MACHINE DOUBLING

Press machine doubling is another common Peace dollar variety. On the Peace silver dollar, most doubled coins are only doubled on the obverse. This suggests that they are due to machine doubling since there would be an equal likelihood of doubled obverse and reverse dies. A 1923-P doubled obverse is definitely from machine doubling since it was the only doubled coin in a mint sealed bag of coins (all 1923-P dates) examined by the authors. In addition, of the several doubled 1922, 1923, and 1925-P coins known for each date, none are identical, which indicates that they are from machine doubling.

It was noted in the discussion of the Morgan silver dollars that one side, the reverse, was predominantly doubled from mechanical play in the press during striking. For the Peace dollar, it was the obverse and it was not the result of a repunched date, since other features were usually doubled.

Looseness in the press die holder and other parts caused the dies to move or shift during the striking process. This resulted in the shelf-like machine doubling. This doubling is slightly different for each coin. Because they are so common, they do not command any price premium.

DIE BREAKS

The Peace dollar dies were generally used longer in striking coins than the Morgan dollar dies. There were also less inspections of the coins so that more errors and die breaks on coins were released. The Peace dollar series has some very spectacular die breaks showing on the coins.

Since the die breaks occurred near the end of the die's lifetime, relatively fewer coins were struck with the defect. Also the die break would begin as a small hairline crack showing on some coins and would progress to a longer die break on later coins as the die continued to deteriorate and chip away.

Small hairline cracks are fairly common on Peace dollars although not as frequent as they were on the Morgan dollars. They are not listed because of this and command no premium to collectors. Die breaks that are readily visible to the naked eye with significant chips out of the die are collectable and do command a premium price. The following is a list of major die breaks:

Major Die Breaks

VAM

1922-P 2A - Break from ear down to neck.
    2B - Break from nose to upper lip.
    2C Vertical break at the back of hair.

Clashed Obverse

Clashed Reverse

VAM
2D - Break below eagle's wing in field.
2E - Horizontal break on eagle's back.
1923-P 1A - Break on back of jaw.
1B - Slanting break at back of hair.
1923-P 1C - Diagonal break from O in Dollar.
1D - Vertical break on cheek.
1E - Diagonal break across eagle's back.
1924-P 1B - Break in middle of wing.
1C - Back of hair.

DOUBLED DIES

It took several blows of the working hub to transfer the design to a working die. Any misalignment of the hub and die during the later blows could cause doubling of some of the design.

There are some significant doubled dies of the Peace dollar series that are visible to the naked eye. The strongest is the 1934-D with strongly doubled Liberty head profile and rear rays in the tiara. There are also doubled rays on the tiara of a 1923-P die that are very visible. A number of other dates have less prominent doubling on the obverse and reverse. The following is a listing of known doubled dies. There also have been reported, which the authors have not seen, a 1927-P doubled obverse and doubled reverses for 1925-P, 1927-S and 1934-D.

List of Double Dies

VAM
1921-P 2 Doubled PEACE letters on left side.
1922-P 3 Doubled leg feather and olive leaves.
4 Doubled motto and designer's initials.
5 Tripled olive leaves and leg feathers.
1922-D 3 Doubled olive branch.
1923-P 2 Doubled tiara rays, designer's initials, TRUST, and lower hair curl.
3 Doubled lower reverse olive leaves.
1924-P 2 Doubled rays above ONE and eagle's back and rear feather of leg.
1925-S 2 Doubled olive branches, leaves, rays and leg feathers.
1926-P 2 Doubled olive branches, leaves, rays and leg feathers.
1928-S 3 Doubled rear rays in tiara, designer's initials, motto and back of hair.
1934-D 3,4 Doubled profile, designer's initials, rear tiara rays, and TRUST.

DOTS

A number of the Peace dollars have round raised dots on their surfaces similar to those found on the 1921 P, D, and S Morgan dollars. These are from tiny gas bubbles trapped in the steel when it was cast. The dots are not from the use of a Rockwell hardness tester of the face of the dies after they were hardened. The size of the dots ranged from two to seven thousands of an inch in diameter and are considered too small and numerous to have been made by a Rockwell hardness tester.

The dates occurred from 1921 through 1924 and no coins show these raised dots from 1925 and afterwards. Presumably the steel for the dies was better made without gas bubbles or from a different source in 1925 and later years so the dots did not show up on the coins.

Some coins only show a single dot on either the obverse or reverse. Some dates show multiple dots scattered over various parts of the coin. The 1924-P has several varieties that show over thirty dots of various sizes on the obverse!

The following is a list of currently known Peace dollar dot coins. Undoubtedly other dot coin varieties exist.

1921-P One dot below ONE on reverse.
1922-P Two varieties with single dots.
1922-D One dot in O of ONE.
1923-P Three varieties with single dots.
1923-D One dot below N of IN.
1924-P 12 varieties with up to over 30 dots on the obverse of a single variety.
1924-S One dot below E in WE.

ROTATED DIES

As with the Morgan dollar, the Peace dollar normally has the obverse and reverse upside down with respect to each other. Some rotations have been found from this position due to the dies positioned incorrectly or working loose in the press. The following is a list of the currently known rotations in degrees:

Year	Rotation
1921-P	20° CCW
1922-P	100° CCW
1922-D	45° – 53° CW
1923-P	25° – 100° CW
1927-D	15° CW

OTHER ERRORS

Some examples of other Peace dollar errors are shown in the accompanying photographs. Several different types of planchet errors are illustrated. The 1922-P

1923-P 75° Clockwise Rotation

has a long split in the planchet from the date to the ear. The 1924-P has a split below the ear. It was caused by impurities lying within the whole thickness of the planchet. A related error is the 1923-P with obverse and reverse laminations. In these cases, the rolling of the silver strip caused the slag impurities to be rolled out in a thin layer just under the surface of the planchet resulting in large laminations.

There are a number of spectacular striking errors in the Peace dollar series. The 1922-P shows a strike through on the reverse, also caused by a strip of metal between the die and planchet. A weak strike is illustrated on the 1924-P. It shows a smooth surface in the hair over the ear.

The Peace dollar series has a relatively greater number of rim clips than the pre-1921 Morgan dollar series. Some examples are shown in the accompanying photos. The clips do not extend much beyond the coin rim. Large clips are extremely rare for silver dollars because of the weight check of the coins at the mints. The 1923-P shows three small clips. Multiple clips are quite rare on silver dollars. The more usual is a single clip like the 1922-P example shown.

Another striking error is the 1923-S partial collar with only part of the edge reeding showing. This so-called "railroad rim" effect was caused by the planchet being partially within the collar when it was struck by the dies.

A related error is the broadstruck 1922-S dollar shown in the accompanying photos. This was caused when the planchet was struck entirely out of the collar by the dies. As a result, the coin has a larger diameter than normal without edge reeding. The authors have also seen a nice 1921-P and 1922-D broadstruck dollars.

Double struck Peace dollars are extremely rare. One example is the 1921-P shown in the accompanying photo. It failed to be ejected from the press after being struck the first time. It was struck a second time after rotating about 10 degrees CW. This second strike obliterated all of the first strike design except for part of the date numeral 1, IN and L of LIBERTY on the obverse and UNITED and ONE on the reverse. The edge of the coin shows two sets of reeding where the coin did not fully drop or was not completely pushed back into the collar.

Another example of a double struck Peace dollar is the illustrated 1922-S. It is one of the more spectacular striking errors of the Peace dollars. This one was struck a second time about 180 degrees rotated from the first strike. The bottom of the obverse shows E and R of LIBERTY from the first strike adjacent to the date numbers. The original strike design was almost completely obliterated from the reverse except for faint rays at 11 o'clock. The second strike was not completely in the collar as shown by the collar's top markings on the lower obverse. Since the first striking of the coin would not fit easily back into the collar, the coin ended up with the lower obverse sitting on top of the collar. As a result, the lower obverse die did not obliterate the first strike design of that part of the coin held up on top of the collar.

The double struck 1923-P is different with a vertical shift between strikings of half a coin width. Also shown is a 1922-S that was struck about 10 percent off center. These two types of striking errors are very rare for Peace dollars and they command large premium prices.

1922-S
Broadstuck

1923-S Tilted Partial Collar

1923-P Lamination

1922-P Split Planchet

1924-P Obverse
Weakly Struck

1923-P Reverse Lamination

1922-P Rim Clip

1922-P Reverse Struck Through

1924-P Split Planchet

1921-P Double Struck

1923-P Triple Clip
(Photo Courtesy of Natalie Halpern)

1922-S Double Struck, Rotated 180°

1921-P Double Struck,
Double Reeding

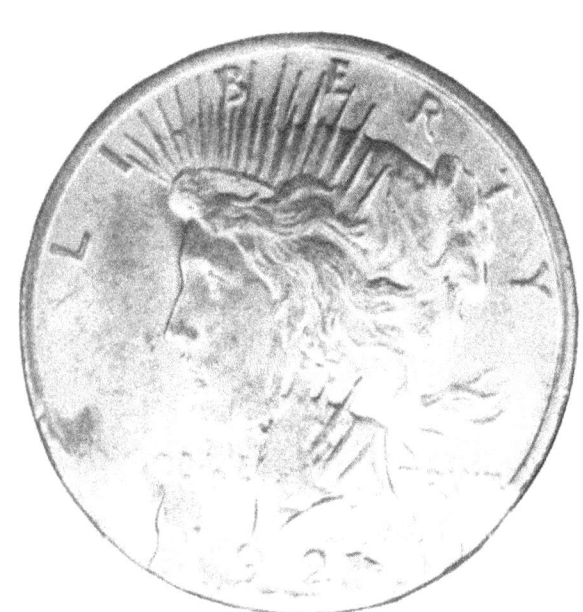
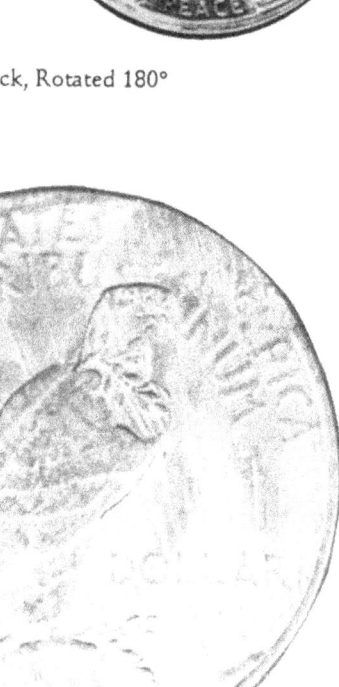

1923-P Double Struck

1922-S Struck 10% Off-Center

Chapter 14

Condition Analysis and List Of Die Varieties

The following is a discussion of condition availability and listing of die varieties for the Peace dollar from 1921 – 1928 and 1934 and 1935. The die varieties are designated by a number, type, and a short description of the main variety feature. There are fewer Peace dollar varieties than Morgan dollar varieties because only one-third as many coins were minted, they were minted for a fewer number of years, and the die making technology was more advanced. This last factor allowed the dies to strike more coins and the date did not have to be punched into each individual working die. Also, the edge reeding in the collar was standardized for all issues at 189.

Nonetheless, the Peace dollar has large variations in quantity minted, fullness of strike, luster, frostiness, and die wear from year to year and mint to mint. It is not as popular with collectors and investors as the Morgan dollar by a wide margin. Many factors contribute to this reduced popularity including more rounded and less sharply detailed design, lack of proof-likes, less frostiness or contrast of the devices, generally a higher percentage of coins with excessive die wear evidenced by "orange peel" or surface roughness, a more modern design which lacks the strength of the more classic Morgan design, and the coins are not as old. Assembling a nice set of Peace dollars can be challenging, but considerably easier and less costly than trying to put together a comparable quality Morgan dollar set.

1921-P

The first year of issue of the Peace dollar is of high relief design. They were struck during the last three days of 1921. Because of the high relief and rushed production, most coins of this date show a weak strike with detail lacking in the hair over the ear on the obverse and lack of detail on the wing feathers over the eagle's right leg on reverse. This lack of high point detail should not be mistaken for coin wear however. A slightly circulated coin will show some wear on the cheek and upper parts of the eagle's wing.

Sliders are common for this date and a coin should always be carefully examined to determine if any wear exists. Tilt the coin under a strong light to see if grayish areas or hairlines exist on the cheek and eagle or in the fields. Its availability from the grading services in MS64-66 is just slightly under the median. That is, it is neither very common nor very scarce in these grades compared with other Peace dollars.

One minor variety shows slight doubling of PEACE.

1	**I 1 • Aa (Normal Die)**	I–1	R–2

Obverse I 1 – Normal die of I type. Detail of hair around ear usually missing even on BU specimens, due to weak strike.
Reverse Aa – Normal die of A type.

2	**I 1 • Ab (Doubled PEACE)**	I–2	R–3

Reverse Ab – Letters in PEACE doubled slightly on left side.

1922-P

Because of the difficulty of striking the high relief design late in 1921, the design relief was made shallower early in 1922. The initial attempt was not entirely satisfactory with the B[1] reverse resulting in slight weakness in the hair over the ear and eagle's wing above the leg. Only a few dies of the B[1] reverse were used at the Philadelphia Mint however, so they are only a small fraction of the large 1922-P mintage. A later modification of the design changed some of the details and the field radius of curvature which allowed more fully struck coins. As a result, weakness of strike is generally not a problem for this year.

Despite the enormous mintage, the 1922-P is more difficult to locate in MS65 condition than the other high mintage date, the 1923-P. It also has a problem with the so-called water spots probably caused by improper washing and drying of the planchets, or later washing and rebagging of contaminated coins.

Its availability from the grading services in MS64 is among the most common, just under that for the 1923-P. In MS65 it is the third most common

1921-P 2 R Doubled PEACE

and in MS66 it is at about the top one-third point in overall availability.

This date has some fairly large die breaks as some dies were used well beyond their normal service retirement point. The very visible die breaks command a significant price premium and are popular collector's items. The 1922-P also has several minor doubled dies and a nice visible die gouge in the high rays below "E" of LIBERTY. These minor varieties are worth only a small premium in price.

1	**II 1 • B^{1}a (Early Design)**	I–3	R–3

Obverse II 1 – Normal die of II type.
Reverse B^{1}a – Normal die of B^1 type.

2	**II 1 • B^{2}a (Normal Die)**	I–1	R–1

Reverse B^{2}a – Normal die of B^2 type.

2A	**II 1 • B^{2}a (Ear Ringed)**	I–3	R–6

Obverse II 1 – Die break causing shaft of metal from ear down to neck.

2B	**II 1 • B^{2}a (Moustache)**	I–3	R–6

Obverse II 1 – Die break from nose to back of upper lip of Liberty Head.

2C	**II 1 • B^{2}a (Extra Hair)**	I–3	R–6

Obverse II 1 – Curved sliver of metal at back of hair due to die break.

2D	**II 1 • B^{2}a (Reverse Field Die Break)**	I–3	R–6

Reverse B^{2}a – Die break in field above DOLLAR causing diagonal sliver of metal.

2E	**II 1 • B^{2}a (Reverse Wing Die Break)**	I–3	R–6

Reverse B^{2}a – Die break on eagle's back causing a raised tear drop of metal.

2F	**II 1 • B^{2}a (Die Gouge in Rays)**	I–3	R–3

Obverse II 1 – Horizontal die gouge in rays below E of LIBERTY.

3	**II 1 • B^{2}c (Doubled Leg Feathers)**	I–3	R–3

Reverse B^{2}c – Lower leg feathers doubled on left side as are left olive leaves and couple of feathers on left edge of eagle's middle left side.

4	**II 4 • B^{2}a (Doubled Motto)**	I–2	R–3

Obverse II 4 – Slightly doubled bottom of WE TR, designer's initials, date digits and lower hair strands.

1922-P 2A O Ear-Ringed Die Break

1922-P 2B O Moustache Die Break

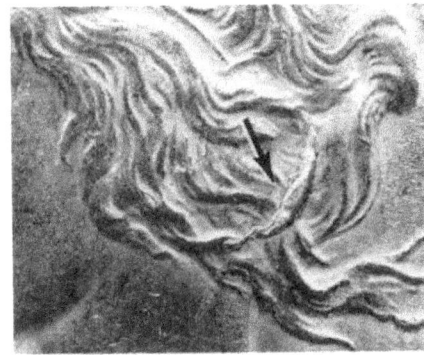

1922-P 2C O Die Break in Hair

1922-P 2D R Die Break in Field

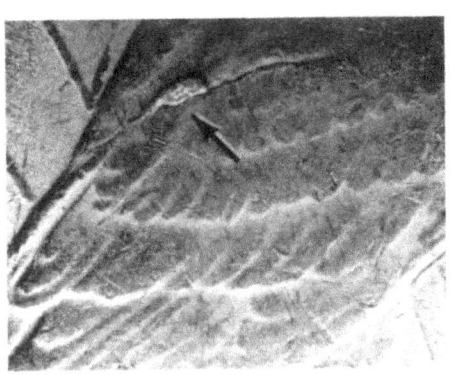

1922-P 2E R Die Break on Eagle

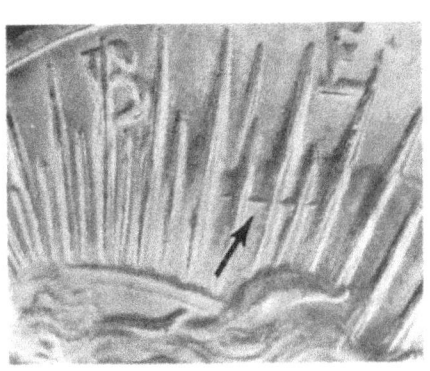

1922-P 2F O Die Gouge in Rays

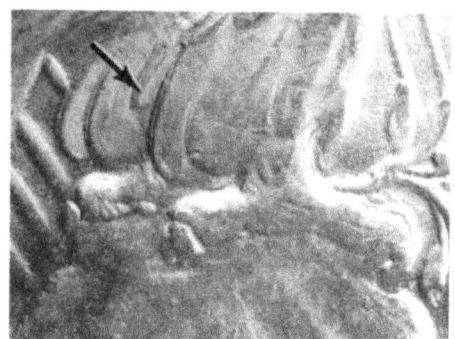

1922-P 3 R Doubled Leg Feathers

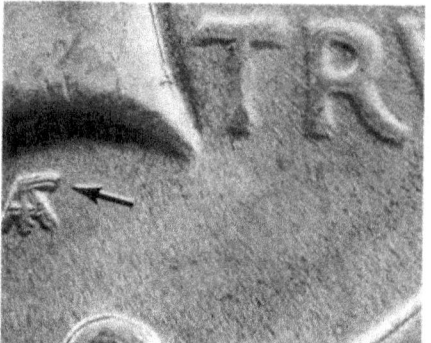

1922-P 4 O Doubled Motto,
Designer's Initials

1922-P 5 R Tripled Olive Leaves
(Photo courtesy of Jeff Oxman)

1922-D

About one-third of the date was struck using the earlier B^1 reverse. These coins are typically weakly struck. Those coins with the later B^2 reverse usually are much better struck.

The fairly high mintage for this branch mint meant some dies were in service excessively long. As a result, the 1922-D shows an above average amount of die cracks and roughness in the field or "orange peel" appearance due to worn dies. The die cracks appear around the periphery and across the neck. They do not affect the value in most cases. It is at about the top one-third point in overall availability from the grading services in MS64-66.

There is only one known minor variety for this date that has small doubling of the olive branch.

1	II 1 • B^1a (Early Design)	I–2	R–2
	Obverse II 1 – Normal die of II type.		
	Reverse B^1a – Normal die of B^1 type.		
2	II 1 • B^2a (Normal Die)	I–1	R–1
	Reverse B^2a – Normal die of B^2 type.		
3	II 1 • B^2c (Doubled Olive Branch)	I–3	R–3
	Reverse B^2c – Doubled lower reverse including left side of olive branch and leaves, rear of leg feathers and rays above olive branch.		

1922-D 3 R Doubled Olive Branch

1922-S

This date is difficult to locate in fully struck MS65 condition. The reason is that about one-half were struck with the earlier B^1 reverse. Although it has a large mintage, apparently large quantities were released into circulation for this first year of issue of the Peace dollar by the San Francisco Mint. Its availability in grades MS64-66 from the grading services is at about the one-third point from the scarcest date.

1	II 1 • B^1a (Early Design)	I–1	R–1
	Obverse II 1 – Normal die of II type.		
	Reverse B^1a – Normal die of B^1 type.		
2	II 1 • B^2a (Normal Die)	I–1	R–1
	Reverse B^2a – Normal die of B^2 type.		

1923-P

This date is the most readily available Peace dollar in mint state even though it has a lower mintage than the 1922-P. It is the most readily available in MS64 and MS65 from the grading services and about on par with the 1925-P in MS66 as the most available for the grade. The problem in finding minimum bag marked Peace dollars is the large and high relief wing of the eagle. It is much more vulnerable to visible bag marks than the more shallow and detailed Morgan dollar eagle.

Some of the early strike 1923-P exhibit frosting in the hair of the Liberty Head and frosting in the feathers of the eagle. When combined with the usual full strike and with a minimum of bag marks, these can be among the most attractive of the Peace dollars. As with the 1922-P, some of the 1923-P show the so-called water spots which can decrease the coin's value depending upon their extent and location.

The 1923-P also has some spectacular large die breaks like the 1922-P. It also has a large but shallow die gouge extending vertically down from the chin. There are two known doubled dies. One doubled die is the second strongest doubled die of the entire Peace dollar series showing doubled rear rays of light in the tiara. This is visible to the naked eye and commands a significant premium but is difficult to locate. The common 1923-P thus has some very interesting varieties.

1	II 1 • B^{2}a (Normal Die)	I–1	R–1

Obverse II 1 – Normal die of II type
Reverse B^{2}a – Normal die of B^2 type

1A	II 1 • B^{2}a (Whisker Jaw)	I–3	R–6

Obverse II 1 – Extra sliver of metal from jaw to neck due to die break.

1B	II 1 • B^{2}a (Extra Hair)	I–3	R–4

Obverse II 1 – Sliver of metal at back of hair due to die break. Several variations of this type die break exist with the metal positioned at various places on the LIBERTY head hair.

1C	II 1 • B^{2}a (Tail on O)	I–2	R–4

Reverse B^{2}a – Die break from lower part of O in DOLLAR extending diagonally down to left.

1D	II 1 • B^{2}a (Whisker Cheek)	I–3	R–6

Obverse II 1 – Sliver of metal on cheek due to die break.

1E	II 1 • B^{2}a (Die Break on Eagle's Back)	I–2	R–4

Reverse B^{2}a – Die break from top left of eagle's wing down across back to middle right wing.

1F	II 1 • B^{2}a (Chin Bar)	I–2	R–3

Obverse II 1 – Vertical bar of shallow raised metal from chin down right side of D motto to top of 1 due to die gouge.

2	II 4 • B^{2}a (Doubled Rays)	I–4	R–4

Obverse II 4 – Rays of light in tiara are doubled on left side with those in rear having strongest doubling. Tops of TR in TRUST, lower back hair curl, rear of neck, and right side of designer's initials are slightly doubled.

3	II 1 • B^{2}b (Doubled Lower Reverse)	I–3	R–4

Reverse B^{2}b – Doubled lower reverse including rays, back of feathers on legs, and olive leaves.

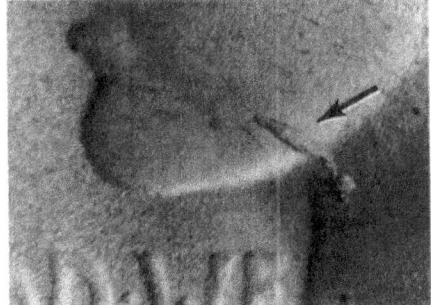

1923-P 1A O Whisker Jaw

1923-P 1C R Tail on O

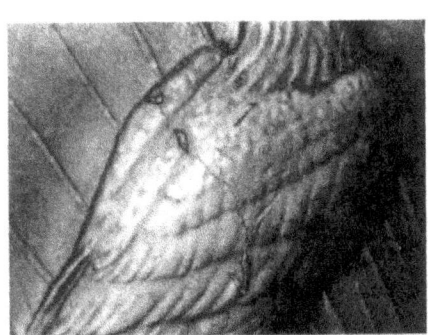

1923-P 1E R Die Break on Eagle's Beak
(Photo courtesy of Bill Fivaz)

1923-P 1B O Extra Hair

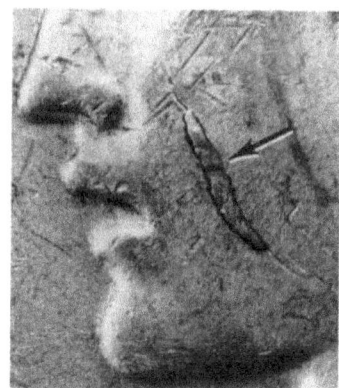

1923-P 1D O Whisker Cheek

1923-P 1F O Chin Bar

1923-P 2 O Doubled Rays, Motto & Hair

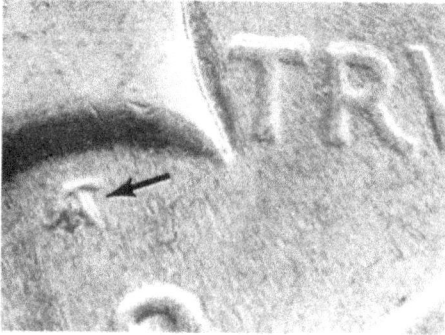

1923-P 3 R Doubled Lower Reverse

1923-D

Locating full strike specimens is not a problem with this date. But is difficult to locate minimum bag marked MS65 pieces. As with the 1922-D, many of the dies were used beyond their normal service life and peripheral die cracks and ones across the base of the neck are common. It is at about the median point in MS64 and 65 availability from the grading services and among the scarcest in MS66.

1   **II 1 • B²a (Normal Die)**   I–1   R–2
      Obverse II 1 – Normal die of II type.
      Reverse B²a – Normal die of B² type with micro I D mint mark.

1923-S

A notoriously difficult date to find fully struck with minimum bag marks. Although the B² reverse was used to strike the entire issue of this date, apparently the strike pressure was very seldom set high enough to bring up the full design detail in the hair over the ear or feathers over the leg. The lower striking pressure extended the die life time for the large mintage. The 1923-S ranks with the 1928-S and 1925-S as the most difficult Peace dollar dates to find of the lower relief design with full strikes. Its availability from the grading services in MS64-66 approaches that of the scarcest dates in these grades.

Only one minor die variety is known with the doubled mint mark on the left side.

1   **II 1 • B²a (Normal Die)**   I–1   R–1
      Obverse II 1 – Normal die of II type.
      Reverse B²a – Normal die of B² type with micro I S mint mark.

2   **II 1 • B²a (S/S Left)**   I–2   R–4
      Reverse B²b – Micro I S doubled on left side.

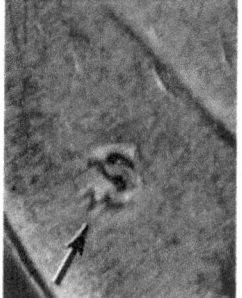

1923-S 2 R
Doubled S

1924-P

This date has a problem with worn dies showing excessive "orange peel" appearance over the fields and devices. Coins struck with worn dies exhibit dull luster and roughness in the otherwise smooth fields. There exist nice fully struck early strike specimens, so locating MS65 coins is not too difficult. This date is about the fourth most commonly available in grades MS64 and 65 from the grading services and about the third most available in MS66.

The 1924-P has some very interesting die varieties. A shallow die gouge exists from the left side of the D in the motto down to 1. There is also a very large die break in the center of the wing. A doubled die reverse shows doubled rays above ONE and top of the eagle's back.

1	**II 1 • B²a (Normal Die)**	I–1	R–1

Obverse II 1 – Normal die of II type.
Reverse B²a – Normal die of B² type.

1A	**II 1 • B²a (Bar D)**	I–2	R–4

Obverse II 1 – Vertical bar of shallow metal from left side of "D" in motto down to left side of 1 due to die gouge.

1B	**II 1 • B²a (Die Break on Wing)**	I–3	R–4

Reverse B²a – Large circular die break in center of wing.

1C	**II 1 • B²a (Die Breaks in Hair)**	I–3	R–4

Obverse II 1 – Two vertical die breaks at back of hair.

2	**II 1 • B²i (Doubled Reverse)**	I–3	R–3

Reverse B²i – Rays above ONE and eagle's back and rear feathers of leg are doubled.

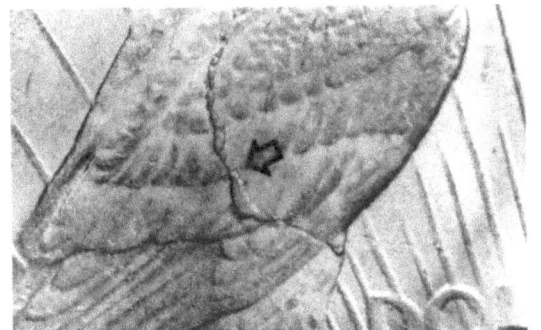
1924-P 1B R Die Break on Wing

1924-P 1A O Bar D

1924-P 1C O Die Breaks in Hair

1924-P 2 R Doubled Reverse

1924-S

A low mintage date which is for the most part weakly struck. Locating a true MS65 coin is very difficult because of excessive bag marks and weak strike problems. It is about fifth or sixth scarcest in MS64-66 from the grading services.

1	**II 1 • B²a (Normal Die)**	I–2	R–2

Obverse II 1 – Normal die of II type.
Reverse B²a – Normal die of type with micro I S mint mark.

1925-P

In general, this date is fully struck with brilliant fields and nice luster. Many 1925-P's have light golden toning on both sides which was probably caused by some contaminant in their storage area at the Philadelphia Mint. In contrast with the 1924-P, the 1925-P seldom exhibits surface roughness due to worn dies. In MS64 it is about the third most available from the grading services; in MS65, the second most available behind the 1923-P and in MS66 about on par with the 1923-P as the most available.

1   II 1 • B^2a (Normal Die)   I–1   R–1
     Obverse II 1 – Normal die of II type.
     Reverse B^2a – Normal die of B^2 type.

1925-S

Another San Francisco Mint coin that is typically weakly struck with excessive bag marks. Therefore, MS65 pieces are difficult to locate. This date is at about the lower one-third point in availability from the grading services in MS65 and among the scarcest in MS65 and 66. There is a doubled die reverse with doubled olive branches, rays and leg feathers.

1   II 1 • B^2a (Normal Die)   I–1   R–2
     Obverse II 1 – Normal die of II type.
     Reverse B^2a – Normal die of B^2 type with micro I S mint mark.

2   II 1 • B^2b (Doubled Olive Branches)   I–3   R–3
     Reverse B^2b – Doubled olive branches and leaves on left side, rear feathers of eagle's legs and rays below olive branches, behind legs and above and below ONE on left side.

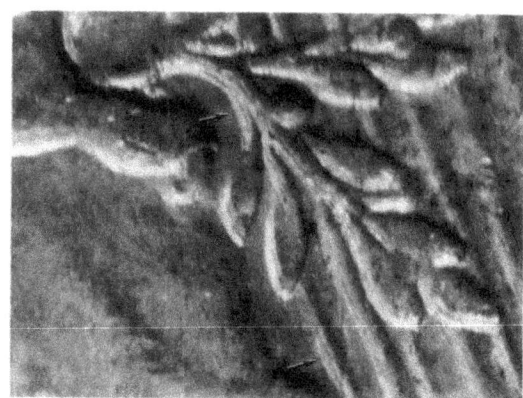

1925-S 2 R Doubled Olive Branches, Rays

1926-P 2 R Doubled Rays & Feathers

1926-P

A relatively low mintage coin which makes MS65 condition fairly scarce. As with the 1925-P, this date typically shows a full strike with good luster and brilliant fields. Some even exhibit the two-sided light golden toning so desirable on the 1925-P. It is at about the top one-third point in availability from the grading services in MS64-66. There is a doubled die reverse with doubled olive branches, rays and leg feathers.

1   II 1 • B^2a (Normal Die)   I–1   R–2
     Obverse II 1 – Normal die of II type
     Reverse B^2a – Normal die of B^2 type.

2   II 1 • B^2b (Doubled Olive Branches)   I–3   R–3
     Reverse B^2b – Doubled olive branches and leaves on left side, rear feathers of eagle's legs and rays below ONE on left side.

433

1926-D

This date is one of the easiest mint mark Peace dollars to find in nice MS65 condition. Most show a full strike with nice luster. Very few show die cracks like the 1922-D and 1923-D due to excessive die usage. It is at about the top one-third point in availability from the grading services in MS64 and 65 and slightly more available in MS66.

A minor die variety shows a D mint mark tilted to the right.

1926-D 2 R D Tilted Right

1   **II 1 • B^{2}a (Normal Die)**   I–1   R–2
  Obverse I 1 – Normal die of II type.
  Reverse B^{2}a – Normal die of B^2 type with micro I D mint mark.

2   **II 1 • B^{2}b (D Tilted Right)**   I–3   R–3
  Reverse B^{2}b – Normal die of B^2 type with micro I D mint mark tilted to right at normal height.

1926-S

Among the best struck of the San Francisco minted coins, this date is not too difficult to locate in MS65 condition. This date is at about the mid-point in availability in MS64-66 from the grading services. Two minor die varieties exist with different placement of the S mint mark.

1   **II 1 • B^{2}a (Normal Die)**   I–1   R–2
  Obverse II 1 – Normal die of II type.
  Reverse B^{2}a – Normal die of B^2 type with micro I S mint mark.

2   **II 1 • B^{2}b (High S)**   I–3   R–3
  Reverse B^{2}b – Normal die of B^2 type with micro I S mint mark set high.

3   **II 1 • B^{2}c (Medium High S)**   I–2   R–3
  Reverse B^{2}c – Normal die of B^2 type with micro I S mint mark set medium high and tilted slightly left.

1926-S 1 R Normal S
(Photo courtesy of Coin World)

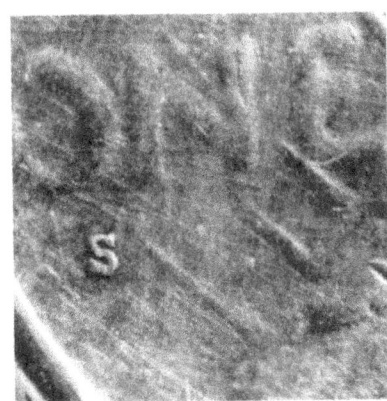

1926-S 2 R High S
(Photo courtesy of Coin World)

1926-S 3 R Medium High S

1927-P

This low mintage date is usually fully struck with good luster and brilliant fields. Because of the low mintage many AU specimens have been saved. Beware of sliders being passed off as BU. Always examine the high points and fields for grayish cast due to wear or hairlines. It is at about the lower one-third point in availability from the grading services in MS64-66.

1   **II 1 • B^{2}a (Normal Die)**   I–1   R–3
  Obverse II 1 – Normal die of II type.
  Reverse B^{2}a – Normal die of B^2 type.

1927-D

Very difficult to locate in MS65 condition, but this issue usually is fully struck with good luster. As a scarce date, many sliders are around and the buyer must be careful when buying BU coins. This date is among the scarcest from the grading services in grades MS64-66.

1 II 1 • B²a (Normal Die)   I–1   R–2
   Obverse II 1 – Normal die of II type.
   Reverse B²a – Normal die of B² type with micro I D mint mark.

1927-S

This date has the typically somewhat weak San Francisco Mint strike although fully struck pieces occasionally can be found. The Redfield hoard contained nice specimens of the 1927-S, making them temporarily available in quantity in the late 1970s. This date is also among the scarcest from the grading services in grades MS64-66.

There is only one variety for this date – an S mint mark set high.

1 II 1 • B²a (Normal Die)   I–1   R–3
   Obverse II 1 – Normal die of II type.
   Reverse B²a – Normal die of B² type with micro I S mint mark.

2 II 1 • B²b (High S)   I–2   R–3
   Reverse B²b – Normal die of B² type with micro I S mint mark set high.

1928-P

Because this is the lowest mintage Peace dollar, it was saved extensively in all grades. The main problem with mint state specimens is a slight weakness in strike for some of them. As with any scarce Peace dollar, sliders abound and the buyer must always carefully examine any offered as mint state to determine if any wear exists on high points or in fields. It is just below the median in availability in grades MS64 and 65 from the grading services and among the scarcest in MS66.

1 II 1 • B²a (Normal Die)   I–1   R–3
   Obverse 1 – Normal die of II type.
   Reverse B²a – Normal die of B² type.

1928-S

It is extremely difficult to locate a fully struck MS65 specimen similar to the 1923-S, 1924-S and 1925-S if not more so. Consistently weak strikes are the major problem of this date. This date is among the scarcest in availability in grades MS64-66 from the grading services.

There are two die varieties of the 1928-S — an S mint mark set slightly high and one with slightly doubled right obverse.

1 II 1 • B²a (Normal Die)   I–1   R–2
   Obverse II 1 – Normal die of II type.
   Reverse B²a – Normal die of B² with micro I S mint mark.

2 II 1 • B²b (Medium High S)   I–2   R–3
   Reverse B²b – Normal die of B² type with micro I S mint mark set at medium high.

3 II 2 • B²a (Doubled Motto)   I–3   R–4
   Obverse II 2 – OD, WE, TR and designer's initials are doubled on right side. Back of neck, back of hair, and right side of rear
   light rays in tiara are slightly doubled.

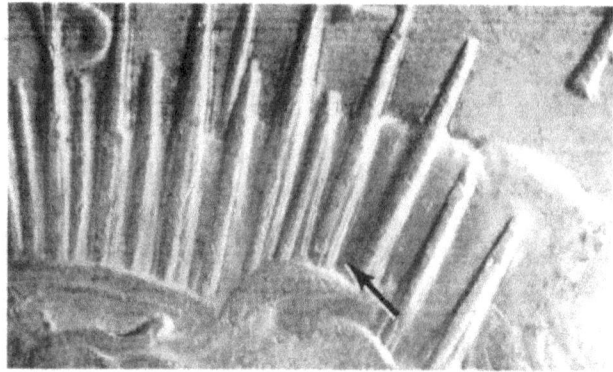

1928-S 3 O Doubled Rays

1928-S 3 O Doubled Motto & Designer's Initials

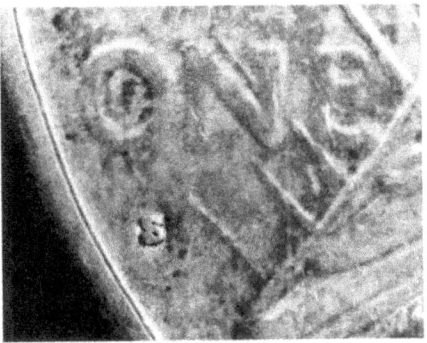

1928-S 2 R Medium High S

1934-P

A relatively low mintage date that is usually well struck. Nice MS65 specimens can be located with enough searching. It is at about the median point in availability from the grading services in MS64-66.

1   **III 1 • B²a (Normal Die)**   I–1   R–3
     Obverse III 1 – Normal die of III type.
     Reverse B²a – Normal die of B² type.

1934-D

A good portion of this date was apparently released into circulation because of the first date of reissue after a lapse of some seven years. Mint state specimens have excessive bag marks so MS65 specimens are fairly scarce. Weak strikes are not a problem with this date. This date is among the scarcest in MS64 in availability from the grading services, at about the median point in MS65 and a little more available than the median point in MS66.

The 1934-D has the most spectacular die variety of the entire Peace dollar series, the doubled obverse. It is very visible to the naked eye with doubled Liberty head facial features, date, motto letters, and the rear light rays of the tiara. This variety is fairly scarce but still readily collectable.

There are two size D mint marks for this date with the larger one being slightly scarcer. Two die varieties show the smaller D mint mark set high and the other with a smaller mint mark tilted to the right.

1   **III 1 • B²a (Normal Die)**   I–1   R–2
    Obverse III 1 – Normal die of III type.
    Reverse B²a – Normal die of B² with micro I D mint mark.

2   **III 1 • B ²b (Medium D)**   I–2   R–3
    Reverse B²b – Normal die of B² type with medium II D mint mark.

3   **III 2 • B²b (Doubled Obverse)**   I–4   R–4
    Obverse III 2 – Doubled forehead, eyelids, nose, lips, and chin on Liberty Head. Motto letters and date digits doubled slightly on right side with WE having large shifts. Rays of light in tiara from midway between B and E back are doubled on lift side with last three having very distinct separate images.
    Reverse B²b – Medium II D mint mark is filled.

4   **III 2 • B²a (Doubled Obverse, Micro D)**   I–4   R–5

5   **III 1 • B²c (High D)**   I–2   R–3
    Reverse B²c – Micro I D mint mark set high.

6   **III 1 • B²d (D Tilted Right)**   I–2   R–3
    Reverse B²d – Micro I D mint mark set at normal height and tilted to right.

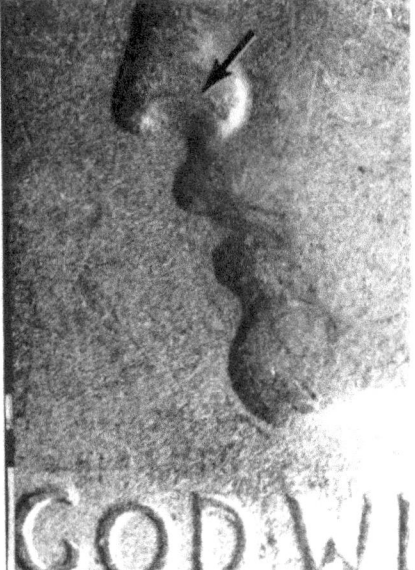

1934-D 3 O Doubled Nose & Lips

1934-D 3 O Doubled Rays

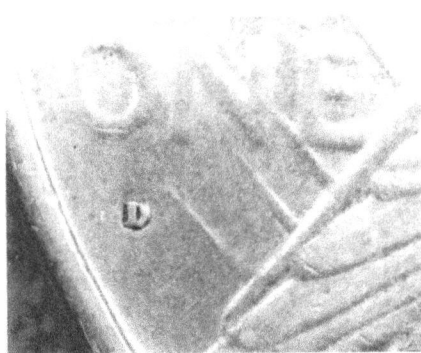

1934-D 5 R High D

1934-D 6 R D Tilted Right

1934-S

This date was also almost all released into circulation like the 1934-D. Mint state specimens are the scarcest and highest priced of all Peace dollars. When located, the 1934-S tends to be well struck for an S mint coin, and nice MS65 specimens can be found. This was the only Peace dollar S mint not in the Redfield hoard. It is about the scarcest in availability in MS64 from the grading services and among the scarcest in MS65 and 66.

The only known die variety shows the S mint mark tilted to the left.

1	**III 1 • B²a (Normal Die)**			I–1	R–2

Obverse III 1 – Normal die of III type.
Reverse B²a – Normal die of B² with micro I S mint mark.

2	**III 1 • B²b (S Leaning Left)**			I–2	R–3

Reverse B²b – Micro I S mint mark leaning left.

1935-P

This date does not have any particular problems with weak strike or excessive bag marks. Even though mint state specimens are fairly scarce, really nice MS65 coins can be located. It is at about the top one-third point in availability in MS64-66 from the grading services.

1	**III 1 • B²a (Normal Die)**			I–1	R–2

Obverse III 1 – Normal die of III type.
Reverse B²a – Normal die of B² type.

1935-S

The strike is usually above average in fullness for an S mint and bag marks are not excessive for the date. This last date in the series is at about the median point in availability in MS64-66 from the grading services.

One die variety shows an added fourth ray below ONE and a seventh added below the eagle's tail feathers. Apparently this was a left over die from 1922 when the design underwent several changes. About one-third of this date show the added rays so it is not a scarce variety and generally commands no premium in price.

Another die variety shows a high micro S mint mark leaning to the left.

1	**III 1 • B²a (Normal Die)**	I–1	R–2

Obverse III 1 – Normal die of III type.
Reverse B²a – Normal die of B² type.

2	**III 1 • B²b (S Leaning Left)**	I–2	R–3

Reverse B²b – High micro I S mint mark leaning left.

3	**III 1 • Ca (Extra Ray)**	I–2	R–3

Reverse Ca – Normal die of C type with micro I S mint mark. Some specimens show a filled I S mint mark.

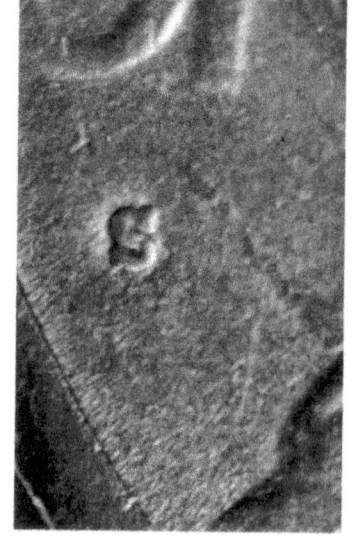
1935-S 2 R High S

Part IV
Working With The Coins

Counterfeit coins can be defined as any coin produced or altered outside the mint. Silver dollars have been counterfeited in the past years for two purposes :
  (1) Common date coins were made for general circulation.
  (2) Scarce coins were made for sale to coin collectors and or dealers.

Of course there is an underlying motive of the counterfeiter; to realize a profit. Hopefully this chapter will better prepare both the dealer and the collector to detect counterfeit silver dollars.

The older counterfeiting purpose was to inexpensively produce a counterfeit coin that would readily pass for general circulation, since the counterfeiter's profit is the difference between the cost to produce the counterfeit coin and the circulation value of one dollar. In as much as silver dollars are no longer in circulation, this counterfeiting purpose is no longer applicable. In the past, however, a number of common date coins were counterfeited and may still be around. Some of these coins were made of debased metal which produced a soft metal coin that was easily scratched and had many design imperfections. Some common date silver dollars were made of high purity silver when the price of silver was very low during the 1930's.

Since silver dollar coin collecting has only become widespread in relatively recent times (for example, after the initial Morgan silver dollar series was completed in 1904), counterfeit coins of numismatic value is a more recent problem. And specifically, altered coins are the primary counterfeiting threat faced by the collector today. The counterfeiter makes his profit from the difference between the cost to produce and the selling price to a coin dealer or collector. Thus, the scarcer and higher priced coins, such as 1889-CC and 1893-S, are more frequently counterfeited to realize a bigger profit.

GENERAL DETECTION METHODS

Table 15-1 is a guide for counterfeit detection. It summarizes the characteristics to look for in the coin's physical makeup, design, field, and edge. Counterfeiting methods fall into three general categories:
  (1) Cast Coins
  (2) False Dies
  (3) Coin Alteration

CASTING COINS has been a favorite method of making counterfeit silver dollars because it is relatively simple and the cost is low. Most cast coins have many surface defects such as weak detail and extra lumps of metal. All cast coins have a different crystalline structure than a struck coin and can be positively identified by X-ray diffraction or microscopic examination.

FALSE DIES can be used to duplicate the mint operations and genuine coins which have been melted can provide the correct metal ingredients. The test for the counterfeiter is then to make as nearly perfect a die as possible. Of all the known methods for making false dies, the cast process is potentially the most perfect. The best cast process consists of casting a ceramic mold directly from a genuine coin which is used to cast a hub, and in turn, is used to make a working die. Little design detail is lost in the metal to metal design transfer from hub to dies. Modern materials and methods allow very good ceramic molds to be made which produce nearly perfect hubs. Counterfeit coins made from the resultant dies can be very difficult to detect. Close examination of the entire coin surface for imperfections is the best detection method.

ALTERATIONS of a genuine coin into one of greater value is another common counterfeiting method and the biggest threat to collectors today. Mint marks can be either added or eliminated; dates can be changed; cuts, scratches, or worn designs can be touched up; and furthermore, two common coins can be mated to produce a scarce coin. All coin alterations depend upon the skill and patience of the counterfeiter. If skillfully done, coin alterations can be very difficult to detect. The close examination of suspect areas with a magnifying glass or microscope is the best method of detection.

The general procedure for detecting counterfeit silver dollars is one of examination in finer and finer detail until all tests of the examiner are passed satisfactorily. Often some small detail of a coin will initially arouse suspicion that the coin is a counterfeit. The coin should then be carefully examined in detail for confirmation that the coin is either counterfeit or genuine.

The following general steps are suggested for the collector in checking their coins:
(1) **Look at the general obverse, reverse, and edge appearance** of the coin with the naked eye to spot any obvious defects such as weak design, large scratches, and extra metal. Many crude cast coins or coins prepared from poorly made false dies can be detected by this initial quick examination. Know the general design features of the coin and compare them with a genuine coin.
(2) **Examine the date digits, mint mark, or mint mark areas** closely with a 10 to 15 power magnify-

Table 15-1 GUIDE FOR COUNTERFEIT DETECTION

CHARACTERISTICS FOR COUNTERFEIT DETECTION

	COUNTERFEITING METHOD	PHYSICAL	DESIGN	FIELD	EDGE
CAST COINS	Sand Mold	Often made of debased metal	Very poor detail	Lumps, streaks, spots, and scratches are frequent defects	Weak detail, incorrect number of reeds, overlapping reeds, reeds missing
CAST COINS	Lost Wax, Ceramic, and Plastic Processes	Weight and size often not within tolerances. Crystal structure not same as struck coin and can be positively identified by X-ray diffraction or microscopic examination	Usually fine detail lost and sharp edges rounded		
FALSE DIES	Hand Cut	Can match genuine coin	Obvious design differences exist	Can be perfect	Can match genuine coin
FALSE DIES	Machine Engraving	Can match genuine coin	Some general loss of detail and some engraving marks	Fine engraving marks usually in circular pattern	Can match genuine coin
FALSE DIES	Impact	Can match genuine coin	Portions of design are weak, broadened and doubled; usually near edge	Can be perfect	Can match genuine coin
FALSE DIES	Spark Erosion	Can match genuine coin	Slight weakening of design details and uniform tiny pits	Uniform tiny pits in some cases	Can match genuine coin
FALSE DIES	Electrochemical Machining	Can match genuine coin	General loss of detail	Can be perfect	Can match genuine coin
FALSE DIES	Powdered Metal	About 5% undersize	General loss of detail and some crushing of design	Some surface roughness	Can match genuine coin
FALSE DIES	Cast	Can match genuine coin	Loss of some detail and rounding of sharp corners. Nearly perfect with use of hub	Lumps, dots, lines, etc. Nearly perfect with use of hub.	Can match genuine coin
COIN ALTERATION	Mint Mark	Perfect if genuine coins used	May not match specific year design	May be rough, raised, or shallow around alteration	Perfect if genuine coins used
COIN ALTERATION	Date				
COIN ALTERATION	Surface		Altered area generally shallow with polishing marks	Altered area generally shallow with polishing marks	
COIN ALTERATION	Split Coin	May be off weight, de-based metal core or copper shell	Perfect if genuine coins used	Perfect if genuine coins used	Fine line somewhere on edge

ing glass. Many of the altered coins can be detected from scratches, polishing marks, and extra metal around these areas or incorrect design date digits or mint mark letters. Compare with a genuine coin or the photographs of date and mint mark types in this book.

(3) **Examine the obverse and reverse design** with a magnifying glass for obvious defects such as lumps of extra metal, weak design, rounded corners where design meets the field, uniform tiny pits, engraving lines in a pattern, excessive polishing, random doubling of design, etc. Again compare with a known genuine coin of same or similar design year. The best detection weapon is detailed comparison.

(4) **Examine the coin edge** with a magnifying glass to see if it has even and distinct reeding. Counterfeit coins often have reeding that is uneven, weak, or overlapping. Split coins usually have portions of the seam which is apparent somewhere on the coin's edge.

(5) **Test the coin's ring.** Balance the center of the coin on the end of a finger and gently tap the edge with a hard object. It should have a clear ring of the correct pitch (basic frequency) and timbre (overtones). Compare the ring with a known genuine coin. Counterfeit coins of incorrect size, debased metal, or split parts will not have a proper ring.

In addition to the above steps, the following are more sophisticated detection techniques which the collector can use for confirmation. Weigh the coin on a balance scale to see if it is within tolerance (412.5 +/- 1.5 grains). Check the coin size (1.5 inches diameter and 0.114 inches thickness). The U.S. Secret Service recommends a simple acid test for silver coins.[1] The acid will blacken a scraped or cut portion of a debased metal counterfeit coin, but will not discolor a genuine silver coin. The acid formula consists of:

Silver nitrate	10 grams
Nitric acid	1 cc
Distilled water	30 cc

These ingredients are available at any drugstore.

If the collector is not completely satisfied as to a coin's authenticity, several courses of action remain. The coin can be presented to a collector friend for an opinion. However, this is not usually satisfactory for a cleverly made counterfeit, since one is apt to receive varied opinions which will still not resolve the issue. Most dealers will also give an opinion on a coin's authenticity if it is presented to them in person. And since the backgrounds of the dealers are varied, one can still receive varied opinions.

The next step is to send the coin to a professional authenticator who will give a written statement of the coin's authenticity for a nominal fee. The American Numismatic Association provides a coin authentication service. Write to the following address for further details on service charges and procedures for sending coins:

> ANA Certification Service
> 818 North Cascade Avenue
> Colorado Springs, CO 80903

Alternatively, the coin can be presented at one of the 70 U.S. Secret Service field offices or sent to the main office at the following address:

> U. S. Secret Service
> 1800 G Street, N. W.
> Suite 239
> Washington, D. C. 20006
> c/o Counterfeiting Office

There is no charge for the Secret Service examination. However, two to three months should be allowed for the examination. If the coin is adjudged to be counterfeit, it will be seized without compensation since possession of a counterfeit coin is unlawful. There will be no prosecution however, unless there was an attempt to knowingly defraud someone. The U.S. Secret Service has the use of several laboratories for examining coins, one of which is located in the Treasury Building in Washington, D. C. Although sophisticated testing techniques are available (such as X-ray diffraction testing), these laboratories rely on detailed examination and comparison of the coin's design for most assessments.

The following sections discuss each counterfeiting methods in more detail. Some photographs are included, which in the authors' opinions, represent some of the counterfeit silver dollar types.

CAST COINS

Cast coins are counterfeit coins made by introducing molten metal into a mold containing the desired design features. After the metal has cooled, it permanently retains the design and shape of the mold. The mold can be made of various materials such as fine sand, plastics, or ceramics.

The primary advantage of cast coins for the counterfeiter is their relative ease of production. The process eliminates the need for large presses, die fabrication, and planchet production. All that is needed is the basic metal (white metal, lead base, or common genuine coins), a means to melt the metal and the mold materials.

Modern materials and production techniques allow counterfeiting high quality cast coins. They can be made of the correct metallic content, proper density, good design detail, clear and smooth surfaces, sharp reeded edges, normal vibration ring, etc: Although the appearances of modern cast coins can be made to closely approach that of a genuine coin, its physical makeup will differ. The metal crystalline structure of a struck coin is disturbed by the flow of metal when it is struck. The metal crystalline structure of cast coins is not disturbed by the cooling process.[2] Thus, a nearly perfect cast coin can be positively identified by comparing its crystalline structure with a known genuine coin. Either X-ray diffractometry or metallographic (binocular) microscope examination can be used for this comparison.[3] These are sophisticated equipment only available at special laboratories. However, the great majority of cast coins can be identified by their size, weight, and design defects.

Mold halves from different coins can be paired to produce rare obverse and reverse combinations without actually possessing the rare coin. For example, an 1890-CC reverse mold could be paired with a 1889-P obverse mold to produce the scarce 1889-CC. New varieties can be created by pairing various design obverse and reverse molds.

Known cast counterfeit coins are listed below. Some of them had weights as low as 286 grains and some were within the weight tolerance of 412.5 ± 1.5 grains.

1878-P, S	1885-P	1901-P
1879-S	1888-O	1902-P
1880-O	1889-P, O (2)	1903-P
1881-P, S	1892-O	1904-S
1883-P, S	1899-O	1921-D, S
	1900 P	1922-D

The following subsections discuss the older methods of making cast coins using sand molds and the newer methods using the lost wax, ceramic, and plastic processes.

Sand Molds

One of the oldest methods of making counterfeit silver dollars is to use a sand mold. This is done by pressing a genuine coin into a container of fine casting sand to imprint the design into the sand. The same procedure is repeated to make the other half of the mold using the other side of the coin (or another coin if desired). The two mold halves are then placed together after passageways have been impressed in the molds to allow the molten metal to enter and allow gases to escape.[4]

Any of several metals can be melted and poured into the molds. After cooling the molds are separated and the extra metal in the passageways are cut and polished off. The seam (formed where the two molds meet) must also be smoothed, and the reeding on the coin edge must be touched up using files or a milling machine.

Since until recently most counterfeits were meant for circulation, the profit margin for the counterfeiter was small for each coin. Therefore, most of the cast counterfeits from sand molds used debased metals such as white metal or a lead base metal. These metals were similar in appearance to silver thus allowing the counterfeit coins to be passed when they were only given cursory examination.

A sand mold produces counterfeit coins with many defects. Since casting sand is relatively coarse in texture, the resulting coin has much design detail lost and a rough surface. The coin's edge will have weak and uneven reeding if touched up by hand. If the reeding was added by using a milling machine, often times the reeding will be overlapping at the start-finish junction. The softness of the debased metal will cause it to have an unusually large number of nicks, scratches, and gouges for its apparent time in circulation. The debased metal will also cause the coin's ring to be dull and low pitched. The contraction of the metal as it cools in the mold will result in the counterfeit coin having a slightly reduced diameter than normal. The light weight of the white and lead base metals will cause the coin to weigh less than standard.

Because of all of these defects, the cast mold is seldom used nowadays to make coins of numismatic value. However, the collector may still come across some of these counterfeit types when examining common date coins.

An example of a cast counterfeit 1883 P silver dollar made from sand molds is shown in the accompanying photographs. Readily apparent is the poor design detail, rough surface, and large gouges on the surface and edges. The debased metal from which it was made causes it to have a very dull ring when compared with a genuine coin.

Modern Processes

Modern cast counterfeit coins can be much more deceptive than those made with a sand mold because of the use of better materials and procedures. One of these more modern processes is known as the lost wax method.[5] A rubber mold is first made of a genuine coin. From that rubber mold several wax replicas of the coin are made. Plaster of Paris molds are made from the wax replicas. After they have dried, molten metal is injected to cast the coin and at the same time vaporize the wax replica. The fine texture of the plaster plus using centrifugal force to inject the molten metal into all parts of the mold produces a counterfeit coin with less surface defects. The first mold of rubber transfers more detail of the genuine coin than casting sand. However, the rubber will not withstand the high temperatures of molten metal necessitating manufacture of the wax core to make the plaster molds.

Other materials may be used in basically the same process as just described above to give even better detail. The initial mold can be made out of plastics or high quality plaster rather than rubber.[6] These molds are then used to make plastic replicas of the coin giving better detail than wax. These replicas are encased in plaster or ceramic material to make the negative mold to cast the

1883 Cast Counterfeit

metal. The molten metal can vaporize the plastic core just as in the lost wax process.

These modern processes can produce cast counterfeit coins with very good design detail, proper metallic content, strong reeding on the edges, normal vibration ring, etc. They must be examined closely to detect any defects. Some of the fine detail is usually lost in the three transfer steps. One should look for rounding of sharp edges in the design; fine lines missing in the hair, eagles wings and wreath; defects in the edge reeding; and bits of extra metal where chips broke off the molds when they were parted from the core. In addition, the coin diameter may be slightly less than normal due to metal shrinkage during the cooling process. As a last resort, crystalline structure examination with an X-ray diffractometry machine or metallographic (binocular) microscope will reveal whether the coin was cast or struck.

The accompanying photographs show a counterfeit 1921-S Morgan dollar made by modem casting processes. The design is shallow, particularly on the obverse. Much of the design detail around the cotton blossoms is missing, and the inner ear fill and part of the ear are also missing. The date digits are rounded where they meet the field instead of meeting at a sharp angle as in a genuine struck coin. The reverse has a large V S mint mark and slanted arrow feathers used on the C⁴ reverse rather than the micro I S mint mark and parallel arrow feathers on the reverse used in 1921. Note also the rounding of the wreath design and letters on the reverse where they meet the field and the numerous dark blemishes on the coin's surface. The edge has overlapping reeding as discussed and illustrated later in the section on the coin edges. In addition, the coin's diameter is slightly less than normal and the thickness is slightly greater than normal, thus producing a higher pitched ring than that of a genuine coin.

FALSE DIES

False dies can be broadly defined as any die of U.S. coins that is not an official product of the mint. For the Morgan and Peace silver dollars, of concern is the fabrication of false dies outside the mint for the purpose of illegally producing coins. These false dies can be made by hand cutting the coin design into the die or by transferring the design from a legal coin to the die using mechanical or electrical means.

There are a number of advantages of false dies to a counterfeiter. The most obvious one is that the false die allows production of numerous counterfeit coins of the same design – more so than the casting method. But perhaps the greatest advantage to the counterfeiter is that false dies can allow almost exact duplication of the mint coin production process thus making counterfeit coin detection very difficult.

The use of false dies allows a coin of the exact

size, weight, metallic content, design, and crystal structure to be produced.[7]

Careful production of the false dies can duplicate almost perfectly the legal coin design. Then, planchets can be made of the proper size, weight, and metallic content. Next, the planchets can be annealed, polished, cleaned, and a raised edge formed on them just as does the mint. These planchets can then be struck from the false dies in presses with a collar forming the reeded edge. In other words, the forger can, with enough attention to detail and with proper equipment, duplicate almost exactly the Treasury process of minting coins.

These false dies also allow counterfeiting of the various mint errors. Off-center strikes, rotated reverses, multiple strikes, clipped planchets, "railroad" rims, thick and thin planchets, etc. can all be counterfeited by duplicating the procedures that caused the mint to accidently produce them.

Additionally, false dies allow the forger to counterfeit rare coins without possessing one. The obverse of one coin can be paired with the reverse of another to make false dies and strike rare or new combinations. For both the Morgan and Peace dollars, the mint marks appear on the opposite side from the date. Consequently, the rare combinations can be counterfeited using common coins. However, unless the forger is careful to select the proper design obverse and reverse from the various Morgan and Peace dollar designs, improper design pairings will readily allow counterfeit detection.

The following subsections discuss the various methods of making false dies and the characteristics that aid in counterfeit detection.[8]

Hand Cut Dies

A straightforward method of producing false dies is to use various hand engraving tools to cut the coin design directly onto the face of the die. The exactness of the copied design depends upon the patience, skill and the tools of the engraver. Because the design of hand cut dies is inexact, the counterfeit coins produced by this method are among the easiest to detect. Detection is merely a matter of comparing the design features with a genuine coin and noting the differences.

The accompanying photographs show an example of a coin from 1890-O hand cut dies. On the obverse, the most obvious difference in the design are the large numerals in the date, elongated 0 in the date, the pointed chin, and the sagging jaw line. On the reverse, the bottom of the eagle's wings curve downward too much, the wing tops are too narrow, the tail feather ends are too far separated and the wreath bow has too large a loop.

The 1888-O counterfeit from hand cut dies is unusual in that it also shows doubling of the motto lettering and date. This is due to the striking process because the doubling shows lines and striations on the

doubled portion from the rough edge of the die where it slid across the coin face. Most collectors can immediately spot a fake from hand cut dies because its overall appearance has a slightly strange impression. Closer examination of lettering will reveal roughness and non-standard design detail.

Machine Engraving

The design of a coin can also be transferred to a die by an engraving machine or pantograph. A tracing tool travels over the coin surface guiding a drill over the face of the die at the same time to duplicate the design. This process is similar to the mint use of the Hill portrait lathe and the Janvier reducing machine as described in Chapter 3. Machine engraving allows more accurate transfer of the design than hand cut dies.

Because the forger transfers the coin design to a false die on a one to one basis, some of the detail is lost in the process. This problem is avoided at the mint by using a large scale model giving a reduction of three to eight times in the transfer process. This reduction allows the required design to be transferred.

Unless the machine engraved false die is carefully polished, fine engraving marks will remain. These will show on the counterfeit coins as spiral marks or some other type of tracing pattern. The other identification feature is the loss of design detail through the rounding of the design edges and general elimination of the finer features of the design.

The accompanying photographs show an example of a coin from 1900-O from machine engraved false dies. There is much detail lacking on the obverse, particularly in the hairlines and cotton blossoms for a coin with this much relief remaining. The machine lines are difficult to show in a photograph of the whole coin, but do show faintly at the top in the field as concentric circles. The detail on the reverse is sharper, but is still lacking somewhat on the wings and lettering.

Impact

In the impact method of producing false dies, the coin to be copied is driven into the die face with sufficient kinetic energy to imprint the design. Various methods can be used to drive the coin into the die face. One method is to use an explosive charge against the outside face of the coin with the inside face placed next to the die. Another method is to mount the coin to be copied on the end of a pivot bar. The bar is then rotated at high speed driving the coin into the heated die face.

False dies produced by impacting a coin have many imperfections. A large coin such as the silver dollar does not impact evenly across the entire die face which results in some portions of the design being weaker than others. The impact tends to spread the coin (especially coins of soft metal like silver) thus broadening some

1890-O Counterfeit Coin
From Hand Cut Dies

1888-O
Counterfeit from Hand-Cut Dies (also shows strike doubling)

design details in the false die, usually in an outward direction.[9] Attempts can be made to touch up these defects by hand engraving. However, careful inspection of the coin design will reveal the imperfections of impact made false dies.

The accompanying photographs show an example of a coin from 1889-CC impact produced false dies. The design is sharp in the center on both the obverse and reverse. However, there is some doubling evident halfway to the coin's edge. Some of the letters and stars are weak with broad shadowy outlines.

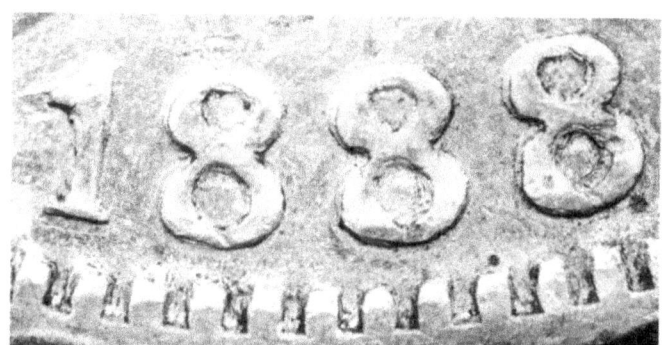

1888-O
Counterfeit Showing Hand Engraved Date
(also with strike doubling)

design. Since metal is also removed from the coin by each spark (although at a lower rate), several coins must be used during the production of one die to maintain the design detail.

Since each spark removes metal from the die in the form of a tiny pit, the resultant die face is uniformly covered by these pits. Low amperage and high frequency sparks minimize the size of these pits. Some of these pits can be removed by polishing, particularly on the field of the die. However, the design can be polished only minimally because it will lose the design detail. Thus, high magnification of the coin design will reveal these tiny pits left in a false die made by spark erosion.

Spark Erosion

Electrical sparks can be used to transfer the coin design to a false die. The coin to be copied is placed close to the die face with a dielectric or nonconductor fluid flowing between them acting both as a coolant and to wash away the metal as the die face is eroded away. Electrical connections are made to the coin and die to cause sparks to pass between them. The sparks jump between the closest points of the coin and die removing metal from the die with each spark. As the metal is removed from the die, the sparks move to the next shortest distance, thus eventually transferring the complete

Electromechanical Machining

Metal can also be removed from a die face by etching using electricity, the reverse of electroplating. The coin is placed close to the die face in an electrolyte or conductive fluid. Electrical connections to the coin and die cause a direct current to pass from the die to the coin and slowly remove metal from the die face. The electrolyte serves as a conductor between the two surfaces and to wash away the dissolved metal. The current and thus the amount of metal removed depends upon the dis-

1900-O Counterfeit from
Machine Engraved Dies

tance between the two surfaces. Because of this, the flow of current will vary across the die face until the complete design is etched out making the distances between the coin and die face equal at all places.

Unlike the spark erosion process which removes metal at the small spark juncture, the electrochemical machining removes metal over a larger area because of the current diffusion through the electrolyte. Thus, the fine design details tend to be lost in the transfer process even though the coin is brought very close to the die face.

Powered Metal

A coin design can be copied directly using powdered metal. The coin is placed in a metal cylinder and powdered metal is added covering the coin design. A plunger in the cylinder is pushed by a hydraulic press compacting the powdered metal. The compacted metal is withdrawn and heated fusing the metal in a sintering process. The false die is thus formed out of the fused metal with the coin design on the end.

Because of the shrinkage during sintering, the resultant false die is approximately five percent undersize. Additionally, the high pressure that is necessary to compact the powdered metal crushes some of the coin design because of the softness of silver. The false dies produced from powdered metal therefore have many imperfections.

Cast

False dies can also be made by casting metal into a mold having the coin design. In the past, cast false dies have been made by using three casting steps. First a wax or plaster intaglio of the coin is made. A transfer is made to a plaster or ceramic positive mold. Molten metal is then poured into this mold to make the cast die.

A more recent method of making cast false dies uses two casting steps and one metal-to-metal transfer step. The refractory ceramic slurry is applied directly onto the coin face. After hardening, the ceramic mold is used to cast a hub (design is raised). After the hub is hardened it is directly impressed into the die face. This method of using a highly accurate metal-to-metal design transfer step replaces a less accurate coin-to-wax or coin-to-plaster step. Better clay materials and methods of using them allows the ceramic mold to be made directly from the coin. It does require a press, however, to transfer the design from the hub to the die.

The older process of making cast false dies using three casting steps usually results in imperfections during the first two soft transfers. The flaking off of plaster or ceramic particles during mold separation causes extraneous raised metal on the coin in the form of dots, lines, etc. In addition, these first two soft transfers lose some of the design detail, particularly the sharp corners and fine lines.

The later method of making cast false dies eliminates a soft transfer step lessening the chances of mold flaking and improving the design detail through the use of a metal-to-metal transfer.

EDGES

The coin edge is, in effect, the third side of the coin and has frequently been neglected by counterfeiters. The collar is used like a third die in producing the reeds on the coin's edge during mint striking operations. If the counterfeiter used false dies, a collar can also be made with the correct number and design reeds by using an automatic gear cutting or milling machine. This will allow the mint operations to be duplicated thus producing a more nearly perfect counterfeit coin. However, the counterfeiter must have access to large presses, milling machines, ovens, etc.; he must obtain the basic materials of steel, silver, mold ingredients, etc.; and he must be knowledgeable in the details of the minting process.

An alternative method of putting reeds on the coin edge is to add them after the coin has been struck. In this case the dies impress the design onto an oversize planchet which is then trimmed to size. The coin is placed into a special machine in which a tool rotates around the coins edge impressing the reeds individually. The difficulties with this method are in obtaining the correct number of reeds, in merging the start and end of the machining, and in setting the machining pressure so as not to cause the coin's edge to be too thick or the coin's diameter too small.

The accompanying photograph shows an example of a 1921-S silver dollar with machined reeding. Clearly evident is the overlapping of the reeding where the machining did not merge together, but rather, it ended up interwoven. This is easily seen by following the reeds in one direction and noticing that they fade out between the reeds of the other direction. The edge of

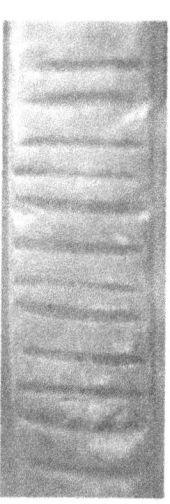 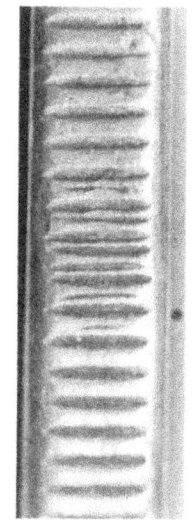

1889-O Counterfeit
Hand Milled Reeding

1921-S Counterfeit
Overlapping Reeding

1889-CC Counterfeit from Impact Dies

this 1921-S silver dollar was also slightly thicker than normal and the coin's diameter was less than normal.

The edge of a cast coin presents the counterfeiter with a problem. To cast a coin, ports are needed in the mold to inject the molten metal and to let gases escape. After the metal has cooled and solidified, these ports contain metal which must be removed from the coin. Since the area where the port has been removed is likely to be rough, uneven, or polished, the ports are usually placed in an inconspicuous area such as the coin's edge. The two halves of the mold also produce a line on the coin's edge where they meet. Thus, a cast coin's edge has usually been touched up by hand at some point. This is frequently detectable from the unevenness of the reeds, varying spacing and depth and roughness of the area.

COIN ALTERATIONS

Counterfeit silver dollars can be made by altering common date genuine coins into scarcer ones. This is an individual coin operation requiring a skillful craftsman and special tools. However, it eliminates the need for the metallurgical knowledge and extensive work required for the preparation of cast coins or false dies. The following subsections briefly describe some of the coin alteration methods.

Mint Mark

Mint marks can be added or removed from silver dollars to increase their worth. This alteration is performed on a lower priced coin of the year of the desired counterfeit coin. The classic example of the Morgan series is to remove the mint mark of an 1895-O to make a counterfeit 1895-P. Some collectors do this just to have something to fill that hole in their coin boards without wanting to make a profit from the sale of the coin. Other common examples are an 1894-O converted to 1894-P, 1901-O to 1901-P and 1928-S to 1928-P. In any case the mint mark can be removed by grinding or cutting it away with jeweler's tools. The area is then polished to remove any tool marks. Close examination of a suspect coin area, where a mint mark was removed, will usually reveal the

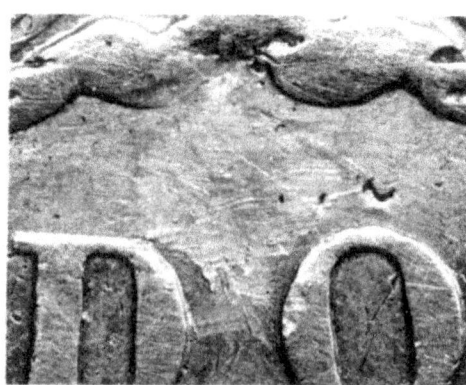

1895 (?) Altered Mint Mark

polishing or tool mark evidence.

Mint marks can also be added to a common date Philadelphia minted coin to increase its value. The desired mint mark is removed from a low-priced branch mint coin and glued or soldered to a coin to be altered. The artistry of the counterfeiter reflects, to a large degree, how much evidence remains of the mint mark addition. Rough edges around the field at the base of the mint mark may remain from the cutting out or soldering steps.[10] A genuine mint mark has sharp corners at this base merging into a smooth flat field. Since there are many different designs of each branch mint mark, sometimes the counterfeiter will attach the wrong mint mark design to a certain year. In some cases a slight prying of a glued mint mark will cause it to fall off.

Mint marks can also be added by cutting away part of the coin's field to form the desired letter(s). In this case the field is lowered around the mint mark and the added mint mark design will not conform precisely to a genuine one. Tool marks may also be evident around the letter(s).

Another method to add a mint mark to a coin is to drill a hole at the mint mark position and insert a plug containing the desired mint mark. The plug is then brazed into place and the seam polished. Usually the plug hole goes completely through the coin. Close examination of the area around a suspect coin mint mark and on the opposite side will usually reveal the seam or polishing marks. The Morgan dollar is hard to plug in this manner since the side opposite the mint mark is within the wheat leaves making it difficult to polish the seam on the obverse.

One of the most common of altered silver dollars is the 1893-S. Many are made by adding the S to an 1893 P by any of the various methods discussed. Other counterfeit 1893-S coins are altered dates as discussed in the next subsection. Mint marks have also been added to the P mint coins to make altered 1889-CC, 1892-S, 1895-S, 1896-S, 1903-S, 1904-S, and 1934-S. Before purchasing any expensive branch mint coin, the mint mark should be closely examined for any tell-tale irregularities.

By far the most serious threat to collectors including those specializing in varieties are the added-on mint marks. The 1896-S shown was certified by ANACS as having an added mint mark. For variety collectors this mint mark should immediately pop out as having a strange shape. It does not conform to the IV S mint mark normal for that date or any of the other known Morgan mint mark designs (I, II, III, or V). Obviously, the counterfeiter fabricated their own mint mark and added it on.

The 1903-S shown is a much more difficult case. Here the mint mark is a type IV S with the proper shape, size and design. The problem is that only V S mint marks were used from 1901 to 1904. So is this a new variety or is it a fake? The field around the mint mark does not have any evidence of tooling marks. Then, the next step

...s to carefully examine all around the edge of the mint mark where it meets the field. There should be a smooth flow of metal from the side of the mint mark down into the coin field. As the microscope photo shows, this 1903-S mint mark has a line where it meets the field along with ragged edges; the sure sign of an added on mint mark.

In examining the edge of mint marks where they meet the field, a hand held magnifying glass of 10 to 15 power will sometimes reveal the edge lines or ragged edges. On more carefully altered coins, a stereo microscope of 20 to 45 power may reveal these details. Sometimes going to a 100 power microscope is necessary. When examining the mint mark, the coin should be held at an angle under the glass or microscope so that the light is reflected off the edge of the mint mark and the vision is aimed directly at the field and mint mark junction. Usually, this requires tilting the coin so its field is at a 45 degree angle to the line of sight. If there is any doubt about the mint mark or date appearance, the coin should be sent to a certification service such as ANACS.

Date

The various altering methods discussed for mint marks also apply to date digits. A digit can be removed from one coin and another digit soldered into place from a second coin. The digit can also be added in the form of a plug. One of the most common methods of date alteration, however, is to cut away portions of a digit to form another one.

Altered dates pose a threat to collectors but fortunately few of these are done skillfully enough to fool those familiar with the dollar date digit designs. The 1893-S shown was altered from an 1898-S and was certified thus by ANACS. The immediate tip-off is the thin center bar of the 3 which is not thick with a blunt end like the normal 1893 "3". This was due to the thin center area of the 8 from which it was made. In addition note that the balls at the top and bottom of the 3 are smaller and do not come together as close as the normal 3. This particular coin had a S/S Right mint mark of the 1898-S VAM 4, further confirming that is was altered from the 1898-S. Variety collectors who recognize unique doubled dates and mint marks have an edge on the normal collector for identifying coins and spotting fakes.

Counterfeit 1889-CC coins have been made by transplanting the "88" from any 1884 to 1889 coin onto an 1879-CC. The date digits are larger for the 1879-CC since they were reduced in size in 1884 for the Morgan series. Therefore, comparison of the "1" and "9" digit size with any 1889 coin will reveal the altered 1889-CC. Similarly, the 1892-S can be fabricated by transplanting a "9" onto an 1882-S. Here again some of the digit sizes will be incorrect. The 1895-S can be made by transplanting a "9" from the 1885-S. Although digits are the same size for the two years, the "5"s are of slightly different design.

Therefore, for any suspect digit transfer coin, check to see if the correct digit size and design are on the coin. Examine closely around the base of the digits where they join the field for any evidence of soldering. There should be sharp corners at the base of the digits merging into a smooth and flat field.

Surface

Strictly speaking, the surface alteration of a coin may not be counterfeiting in its true sense. In most cases surface alteration is performed to upgrade a coin by removing scratches and bag marks or by reducing the apparent wear. The coin will thus bring a better price. Or in some cases the field of the coin will be polished in the hopes of passing it off as a proof coin. Thus, for these

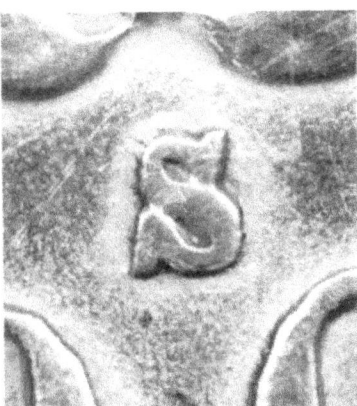

1896-S
Added S
Mint Mark
to 1896-P

1903-S
IV S Mint
Mark Added
to 1903-P

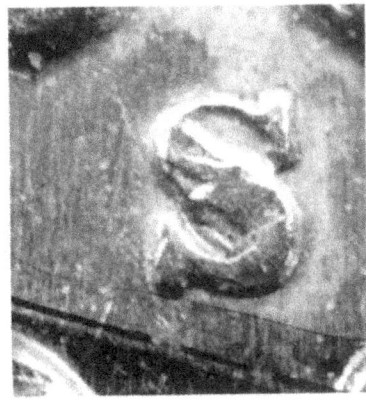

1893-S
Altered Date From 1898-S

cases the collector may be deceived about the coin's condition but not as to year or mint mark.

The various tools useful for surface alteration include engraving, jewelers, and honing types. In all cases, the tools must be used by a skillful artisan for best results. Engraving and jewelers tools can be used to work and polish metal around deep scratches to remove them. Honing can make the coin's surface change shape without removal of metal. This process is known as jet, vapor, or wet honing and consists of an air jet blowing a liquid containing tiny grit.[11] Spherical glass beads is a very effective grit for smoothing a coin's surface.

Split Coin

A scarce coin can be fabricated by joining the obverse and reverse of common coins together. Since genuine designs are used for both obverse and reverse, the coin can appear to be perfect. However, as with other types of counterfeits, the key to detection is knowing what to look for from knowledge of the counterfeiting methods.

Fabrication of a split coin consists of machining or filing down the surface of two genuine coins until their combined thickness is within the required tolerance. The desired date and mint mark (or lack of one) from these two coin halves are combined by soldering. A seam appears on the coin rim which the counterfeiter must attempt to hide by filing and polishing. The milled edges of the Morgan and Peace dollars makes this difficult to achieve.

A variation of the split coin is to hollow out one coin and drop in a different design. The two parts are soldered together with the seam not in the center of the reeding, but at the edge making it more difficult to spot.

Split coins can also be fabricated from electrotype shells. The obverse and reverse shells are made of thin copper built up by an electrolytic process from genuine coins.[12] The design is thus reproduced accurately for both the obverse and reverse. These two shells are placed over a whole metal core or a ground down genuine coin of correct thickness and weight. For counterfeit silver dollars, the copper shells are silver plated. The coin rim still poses a problem for the counterfeiter since at least one seam must be somehow hidden. Variations of the electrotype counterfeit include using a genuine coin for one side and an electrotype shell for the other.

Since all split coins have a seam where the parts were joined together, examination of the coin's edge will usually reveal portions of the seam line. In some cases careful plating and polishing can make this seam difficult to detect. One sure test of a split coin is to listen to the coin's ring. Balance the center of the coin on a finger and gently tap the coin's edge with a hard object. Split coins will not ring at the correct pitch (basic frequency) or have the same timbre (set of overtones) as a genuine silver dollar. It usually helps to compare the suspect coin's ring with that of a known genuine coin of the denomination.

Selected Bibliography

1. Taxay, Don. *Counterfeit, Mis-struck and Unofficial U.S. Coins.* New York: Arco Publishing Company, 1963. (A comprehensive guide on counterfeiting methods and their detection.)
2. Newman, Eric P. "Hobby Must Regulate Its Own Field, Expose Fakes." *Coin World,* March 24, 1965, p. 18. (Discusses counterfeiting methods and their detection. Presented at Professional Numismatists Guild educational forum, Chicago, 1965.)
3. Taxay, Don. "Modern Counterfeiters Directing Activity Toward Faking Rare Coins." *Coin World,* April 7, 1965, p. 65. (Describes various counterfeiting methods. Presented at Professional Numismatists Guild education forum, Chicago, 1965.)
4. Ford, John J., Jr. "Knowledge Only Effective Weapon Against Counterfeits." *Coin World,* April 7, 1965 , p. 24. (Discusses some frequently counterfeited coins and methods used to produce them. Presented at Professional Numismatists Guild educational forum, Chicago, 1965.)
5. Welsh, David E., "Skill Applied to Altering Coins Requires Exact Knowledge of Methods." *Coin World,* April 21, 1965, p. 76. (Describes methods of altering coins.)
6. Newman, Eric P., "Numismatics Faces Major Problem as Coin Forgery Nears Perfection." *Coin World,* November 15, 1967, p. 34. (Describes various methods for producing counterfeit coins. Presented at the International Numismatic Congress, Copenhagen, Denmark, August 28, 1967.)

Footnotes

[1] U.S. Department of the Treasury, U.S. Secret Service, *Know Your Money,* 1966, p. 11.

[2] Eric P. Newman, "Eric P. Newman says Hobby Must Regulate its Own Field, Expose Fakes," *Coin World,* March 24, 1965, p.18.

[3] Don Taxay, *Counterfeit, Mis-struck, and Unofficial U. S. Coins,* Arco Publishing Co., New York, 1963, pp. 53 and 56.

[4] Ibid., p.32.

[5] Ibid., p. 33.

[6] Newman, *Coin World,* March 24, 1965, p. 18.

[7] Eric P. Newman, "Numismatics Faces Major Problems as Coin Forgery Nears Perfection," *Coin World,* November 15, 1967.

[8] The principal source consulted on the preparation of the various types of false dies was Newman's article in the November 15, 1967 issue of *Coin World.*

[9] Taxay, p. 48.

[10] David W. Walsh, "Skill Applied to Altering Requires Exact Knowledge of Methods," *Coin World,* April 21, 1965, p. 76.

[11] Newman, *Coin World,* November 15, 1967, p. 34.

[12] Taxay, p. 48.

Chapter 16

Silver Dollar Preservation And Storage

Silver dollars over the years have been subjected to all sorts of use and abuse. Business strikes were, of course, meant to be used in commerce and little care was taken to preserve them over their 50 to 100 years existence by Government workers or the general public. After being struck at the various mints they were all placed in canvas bags of 1,000 coins to be weighed, accounted for, and shipped. During handling and shipment the coins jostled against one another picking up scratches, digs and slide marks (so called bag marks). Just picture bags of dollars being banged around in stiffly sprung stage coaches or wagons over pot-holed and rutted trails of the nineteenth century and the poor dollars at the bottom of a 60 pound bag! Or being tossed around onto platforms and into vaults. It is a wonder *any* survived in MS 65 condition.

The cloth of the canvas bags contained sulphur compounds which would readily tarnish any silver coins that were against the canvas for any length of time. Over many decades in a bag, dirt and dust could seep through the canvas to coat the coins. So just because coins have come directly from a mint sealed bag does not mean they will all be in a state of preservation just as they were struck from the mint press.

Once the bags were opened for commerce at a bank or by individuals their fate could take many turns. They may have been piled loosely in a cashier's drawer or in someone's desk to pick up more nicks and scratches. Many were placed into 20 coin rolls with wrappers of paper. The sulphur in the paper could cause toning of the coin edge or coin obverse or reverse if it was against the paper.

Fortunately most of the Morgan and Peace dollars remained in bags of 1,000 coins until recent times, mid-1960's and onward. Silver dollars were for the most part disliked and unused by the public. These coins generally received a minimum of surface damage and contaminants. Many coins, however, reached circulation where handling, bouncing in pockets and purses, and sliding on gambling tables and the like wore the coin. There are even dollars with a hole in the middle from a bullet!

It was not until the collector/dealer/investor acquired the coins that any thought and effort for their preservation was given.

HANDLING SILVER DOLLARS

The preservation of silver dollars begins with the proper handling of the coins. Ideally they should be handled using cotton or polyethylene gloves by only their edges. Wearing gloves is not very practical for most people and are awkward to use by many. They are really only needed as an extra safety precaution when handling the most expensive or delicate proof coins.

Silver dollars like other numismatic coins should only be handled by the reeded edges where contaminants and toning are not very noticeable. Grasping the coin carefully between the thumb and forefinger is the accepted method for holding a coin for examination and transfer between viewers. Care should be taken that the coin is not accidently dropped on a table top or floor as a rim dent will likely result.

Above all, do *not* hold or even brush the thumb and forefinger against the obverse and reverse surfaces. The oils in the fingers when left on the coin's surface will etch a series of parallel white lines otherwise known as a finger print. No amount of later cleaning will remove the finger print since the metal will have been permanently etched. Buyers generally shun dollars with visible finger prints which of course lowers their value.

Avoid coughing or sneezing on the dollars since the particles from the mouth can cause permanent spots on the surface. Also, tobacco smoke has undesirable chemicals in the particles and smoke should not be directed towards a coin.

REMOVAL OF CONTAMINANTS

Before silver dollars are stored, one has to consider whether any surface contaminants should be removed. When in doubt, it is best *not* to remove any surface contamination or clean the dollar. Improper cleaning of a coin can be worse than no cleaning at all in most cases and can result in a drastic reduction in value. One of the worse cases of Morgan dollar abuse in a cleaning attempt was the very first Morgan dollar business strike of the President Hayes' specimen. It was struck from brand new dies on a polished planchet. But over the years the family members or museum curators in a well meaning attempt to remove tarnish caused by the coin resting in a cardboard and felt-lined holder stamped No. 1 have unmercifully polished the surfaces until this pedigreed coin is now in AU condition!

Which leads to the first rule of cleaning, never use anything abrasive such as silver polish or other things such as baking soda to polish silver dollars. Removal of contaminants does not mean to also polish or disturb the silver surface.

Dirt

But what kind of surface contaminants are there

on uncirculated silver dollars? The most common is *dirt* and *grease*. Usually this is in the form of a light coating on uncirculated coins. Generally, this will not pose any further damage to the coin since the surface will have probably oxidized and stabilized. Occasionally, the dirt coating may be fairly heavy or spotty detracting from the appearance of the coin. It may also be likely to cause some form of corrosion or pitting. This coating should be removed from the coin to improve its preservation and appearance.

The safest way to remove this from the silver dollar is with a neutralizing solvent that will not attack the silver-copper mixture of the dollar. One such solvent is Trichlorotrifloroethane marketed by E & T Kointainer Co. Another is marketed under TEST-N-SAFE brand. Acetone is another dirt and grease solvent. It is not as safe as the above mentioned products as it may leave some residue if the coin is not rinsed thoroughly after application of the acetone. However, it is readily available as finger nail polish remover.

If the coin is entirely coated with dirt and grease it will have to be dipped in the above solutions following the kit instructions. If the contaminant is localized then a cotton swab on a stick or Q-tip swab can be gently used to clean a small area.

Toning

Toning is the second most common contaminant. It can appear as a small crescent, only on the edge, or over all of one or both sides. It may be a very light delicate shade, multicolored or dark. Generally, the light or colored shades are attractive and desirable. The grey, spotted or dark toning are usually not attractive and therefore can lower the coin's value. Toning is usually a thin film of oxidized silver in combination with another compound, usually sulphur. The thin film results in light interference layers that produce various colors. Other types of toning have colors of the compounds of the oxidized layer. Light attractive toning will usually not further alter the oxidized surface and should not be removed in most cases. Heavily, unattractive toning can pose a danger to the surface and in many cases it is better to remove it for safer coin preservation and to increase its value.

Neutralizing solvents in many cases will not remove toning, particularly the dark and heavy. The oxidized layer has to be removed. This requires a light acid bath that chemically removes the oxidized layer. There are many silver dips on the market. They consist of a chemical, thioura and small amounts of sulfuric or nitric acid. Obviously, this solution can react with the silver-copper metal as well as the oxide layer. So, these silver dips have to be used carefully. The coin should be immersed in the solution only a few seconds and immediately thoroughly rinsed in water. This can be followed by using a neutralizing solvent to be sure the surface is completely clean of all chemical residue.

If a neutralizing solvent is not used, then the water must be removed from the coin surface or water spots can result if the coin is left to dry on its own. The best way to dry the coin is to use a hair dryer to quickly evaporate the water. Or a clean soft towel can be used by gently patting the coin surface (do not rub as hairlines may result).

Carbon Spots

Another contaminant is the so-called carbon spots. These appear as black or dark grey spots with usually a dark core and lighter toned rings surrounding the core. The core is usually a small spot of impurity that is imbedded or etched into the coin's surface. Some of these spots are due to a speck of impurity in the metal when the silver ingots were cast. Others are a contaminant that got between the die and planchet when the coins were struck. And some are contaminants that got on the coin surface after it was struck. They generally have the characteristic of reacting with the silver-copper coin metal and growing in size over a period of time.

These carbon spots can sometimes be removed by dipping in a neutralizing or silver dip. If that does not work then a cotton swab or wooden toothpick can be used to dislodge the impurity. However, it may leave a pit in the surface, but at least this should not be active and growing. If this still fails then there is not much that the average collector can do to remove the spots. At least the dip may have removed the toned ring around the spot but this may appear again in time.

Impure Metal Streaks

Another form of contaminant is the impure metal streak. It appears as a dark rough area on the coin's surface. This impurity is the melt slag that had become trapped in the cast silver ingot. During the preparation of the melt in a furnace, graphite, lamp black or charcoal was placed on top of the molten metal while it was being heated and mixed. This was to protect the melt surface from the oxygen in the atmosphere. The lighter impurities also rose to the surface of a melt. When the melt was poured into an ingot mold, most of these impurities and charcoal (known as slag) remained in the bottom of the melt crucible. Some impurities were poured into the ingot mold where they again rose to the surface or end of the ingot which later got cut off. However, at times small amounts of this melt slag became trapped inside the ingot. When the ingot was later rolled out into a strip, these slag spots become flattened and elongated to become impure metal streaks. If they were on the coin's surface then they would be visible as dark areas. If they were just below the surface of the coin metal then sometimes they would cause a thin layer of metal to be detached or loose in the form of a metal lamination.

Since the impure metal was in place of the silver-copper metal, the black area is imbedded in the coin's surface. These impurities cannot usually be removed very easily. Dips will not phase them since they are a thick layer of impurities. Besides, if the impurities were removed, then what would be left would be a rough depression. This is not very desirable since it has an artificial looking appearance. It is best to just leave the impurities since nothing much can be done with them.

Wood

Occasionally little flecks of wood will be found embedded in the surface of the coin. This seems to be more prevalent for O Mint coins. Most of the time they can be dislodged using a cotton swab dipped in solvent or a wooden toothpick. However, their removal will leave a depression in the coin's surface since these chips were struck between the planchet and die. The chips came from the planchets being dried in a revolving riddle with sawdust after they had been whitened or cleaned in a weak sulfuric acid bath and rinsed in boiling water. Again, most of the time it is best to leave the coin alone and not try to remove the wood flecks.

Circulation Grime

Circulated coins, of course, are coated to varying degrees with dirt and grease or grime. Removal of all of this coating will result in an unnatural appearing coin which is instantly recognized as being cleaned. The best advice is to leave the coin in its natural state and not to clean it. There are a couple of exceptions to this rule however. If the coin is exceptionally dirty and dark looking, then it may help to remove just part of the dirt coating. This must be done evenly so as to not give the coin an unnatural cleaned look. In this case a quick immersion in a neutralizing solution or silver dip will remove some of the dirt coating. This should be followed by a thorough rinse in warm water followed by carefully drying. The slightly cleaned coin will be more natural looking, plus more sanitary and pleasant to handle. Alternately, a cotton swab with acetone can be used to remove some of the excessive dirt and grease.

Another reason to remove the dirt and grease is to study and identify die varieties. To detect many of the coin varieties such as doubled dates and mint marks, the areas must be free of most dirt and grease. For example, it takes only a thin dirt coating to hide the fine details of the 1900-O/CC. Some details caused by a doubled or dual hub die, such as doubled stars and letters, are almost impossible to detect under the normal circulation grime. In these cases it is best to remove some of the grim in local areas around the date, mint mark, stars or lettering using a Q-tip or cotton swab that has been saturated with acetone. A few light passes with the Q-tip will remove much of the grime to allow close examination with a magnifying glass.

Proofs

Proof Morgan dollars were sold by the Philadelphia Mint in paper envelopes via the mail or over the counter. Probably over 90 percent of Morgan proofs with original uncleaned surfaces are toned because of storage in these paper envelopes. Most of this toning consists of light shades of various colors on the coin's delicate surfaces. The toning is usually very attractive and should not be disturbed. Unfortunately, the majority of Morgan proof dollars have had their surfaces slightly scratched, rubbed or cleaned in some way. This shows up as hairline scratches or shiny high points on the coin. Their owners, in a well meaning attempt to remove toning, may have lightly rubbed the coin with a cloth which inevitably produced hairlines. Also, the insertion, removal, or sliding around in paper envelopes could produce hairline scratches on the frosted mark-free devices and smooth mirror fields. It only takes the slightest touch or rubbing to make hairline marks on the delicate proof surface.

Since Morgan proofs are normally naturally toned from being stored in mint paper envelopes, an untoned proof is the exception. Therefore, the toning on proofs should not be removed using silver dips. They should be left toned. In some rare instances, obvious surface contaminants should be removed using only a neutralizing solvent.

Storage

Methods for storing silver dollars have changed considerably over the years. Most of the uncirculated Morgan and Peace silver dollars spent the majority of their existence in mint and bank canvas bags of 1,000 coins. It is only since the early to mid-1960s that many of these bags were opened and dispersed. Coins in these bags were relatively safely stored as long as the bags were not moved and as long as the coin was not against the canvas. Of course, dirt and moisture could easily permeate the canvas.

Nineteenth and early twentieth century collectors most often kept their collections in paper envelopes with notations on the outside. The sulphur in these envelopes inevitably toned the silver dollars, especially if they were uncirculated. Those collectors who could afford it kept their collection in wooden cabinets with trays lined in velvet, felt or pure cotton. The coins were left exposed to the airborne contaminants of the atmosphere. The coin was free to slide on the cloth when the drawer was opened or closed which could introduce slight wear or "cabinet friction" on the coin's high points.

Early collectors also had available "anti-tarnish tissue" which was free of sulphur as well as sulphur free paper envelopes. A dollar wrapped in this tissue paper and placed in a paper envelope would still be somewhat open to the atmosphere and if the tissue rubbed against the coin surfaces it would produce hairline scratches.

Bulk Storage

Silver dollars stored in canvas bags should be removed and stored in rolls of 20 or in individual holders. This is to prevent further tarnishing and accumulations of bag marks on the coins.

Rolls were originally wrapped in paper sized for that purpose. But the paper could add tarnish and did not seal the coins from the atmosphere. The plastic tube became available in the early 1960's which was airtight and made of inert polystyrene plastic.

Early tubes were rather thin which could crack and the lids did not always lock tightly in place. More recent tubes have thicker plastic with secure screw type lids. The safest and most secure tubes are square and made of a white opaque polyethylene. They are chemically inert and will not crack easily.

The coins should not be loose in the tube where they can bounce against one another. The tube should have polyethylene material such as a polyethylene envelope or a piece of saran wrap placed on top of the roll to act as a spacer against the top coin and lid.

Holders

Paper envelopes used by early collectors hid the coin. Every time the coin was to be examined it had to be removed from the envelope which was inconvenient and exposed the coin to handling and rubbing against the envelope. In the 1950's 2 x 2 inch cardboard holders lined with thin mylar or cellophane windows became available. The two halves were folded over the coin and stapled together to enclose the coin. The windows allowed both obverse and reverse sides to be visible. However, for silver dollars there was not much cardboard area to make notations. Unless the staples were crimped flat with pliers they could tear the windows and scratch the adjacent coins when inserted or removed from boxes. In addition, the paper dust particles from the cardboard tended to stick to the windows because of static electricity and be pressed against the coin when the holder was stapled shut. These particles could cause local corrosion spots and toning on the coin surface. These holders are not airtight and dollars tend to tone around the edges if they are stored in them for any length of time. Cardboard holders are not recommended and fortunately, their use has fallen off in recent years.

Over the years various types of holder designs made of inert polystyrene have been available. One type consisted of a recessed round central ring to hold the coin and a square sliding window to enclose the coin. A paper ring surrounded the enclosed coin for notations. It was not completely airtight and one had to be careful not to scrape the coin high points when closing the window. It is not generally available at present. Another polystyrene holder still available consists of two halves that snap together. It is not airtight and notations can only be made using stick on labels. A recently introduced polystyrene holder under the market name "Air-Tite" consists of two round halves that snap together and an inner black neoprene rubber seal. It is safe but has no area for notations and is somewhat difficult to get apart.

Acrylic or lucite holders have been available for some time, both for individual coin holders and albums. It is a safe inert plastic and usually consists of a center section with a cutout for the coin and two outside square windows. The three sections screw together to provide an airtight holder. It is somewhat bulky with raised screws on some brands. Again notations must be on separate labels or cards.

In the mid-1960's the so-called 2 x 2 flip became available. It consisted of two pockets joined together made out of polyvinyl chloride plastic. The coin was inserted in one pocket and a card with notations in the other pocket. When folded over the coin was visible through the clear plastic, no staples were needed, and it was free from cardboard dust. Although not airtight, it was convenient and compact for storing individual coins and became the most popular type of holder.

Much has been written in recent years about the unsafe properties of polyvinyl-chloride or PVC plastic. The stabilizer and softener chemicals in PVC can be

Roll Tubes for Silver Dollars

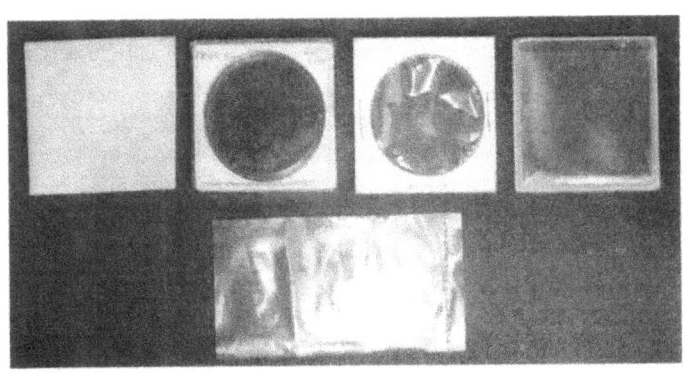

| Paper Envelopes | Plastic with Slide Cover | Cardboard 2 X 2 | Vinyl Flip |

Polyethylene Envelope

released over time and under the right heat and humidity conditions. This can coat the coin and leach out the copper in the alloy to form a so-called green slime. In addition, as the PVC breaks down with time hydrogen chloride gas is released which,

Snap-together Polyethylene   3-Part Acrylic

Kointain   Air-Tite

Storage Boxes

under humid conditions, forms hydrochloric acid and etches the coin's surfaces. Silver dollars have been stored for ten years or more in vinyl flips with no visible damage. On the other hand, a green coating can develop on the coins in less than a year. Vinyl flips are manufactured in various chemical formulations and some are safer for coin storage than others. However, to be on the safe side, silver dollars should not be stored alone in vinyl flips for long periods of time.

Flips made out of an inert mylar (a polyethylene derivative), under the trade name "Saflip", became readily available in the early 1980's. They are somewhat more expensive than vinyl flips. Their stiffness makes them harder to handle in displaying and stacking coins. Also, the plastic scratches and splits easily as the coins are inserted or removed from the flip. They are, of course not airtight but the plastic will not chemically damage the coin. The hardness of the plastic does pose a greater potential for physical damage to the coin from the plastic edge and from the coin sliding about inside the pocket.

There are several ways to encapsulate the coin in safe materials before placing it in a flip. Polyethylene envelopes that are chemically inert have been available for many years. Once the coin has been inserted into the envelope, the top can be folded over to make it relatively airtight. The envelope can be stapled to a paper envelope with notations which was a fairly common storage method years ago. Unfortunately, the polyethylene envelopes are somewhat cloudy and thin, thus not providing as clear a view of the coin as the crystal clear vinyl flips nor as much mechanical protection.

The coin in a polyethylene envelope can be inserted into a flip pocket to give it greater mechanical protection and ease of handling. But the folded polyethylene envelope is somewhat difficult to insert and withdraw from the flip and the multilayered and wrinkled polyethylene envelope hides much of the coin detail, so it must be withdrawn from both the flip and envelope to

be examined. This can unduly expose the coin to physical mishandling and to contaminants.

Another way to encapsulate the coin that has been available since the 1950's, (only heavily promoted since late 1970's) is cast triacetate holders in the form of coin shells. These are marketed under the trade name "Kointain" and consist of two round halves that fit together giving an airtight seal and are snug against the coin edge. The two halves are slightly convex so that they do not touch the coin's surfaces. The plastic is inert and rigid giving good coin protection and safe storage. The two halves are somewhat cumbersome to fit together and pull apart. Also, the plastic has a slight grayish cast which subdues the silver dollar luster and proof-like qualities. Still, for long term storage, a silver dollar in a "Kointain" holder and placed in a mylar or vinyl flip is very convenient and safe.

Individual flips can be best stored in either single row or double row boxes available for the 2 x 2 inch holder. Double row boxes hold about 200 flips while single row boxes can be obtained in various sizes that hold from 30 to 100 coins. When transporting flips in these boxes the flips should be tightly packed together so the coins will not slide around inside the flips as the boxes are jostled and handled. Spacers of foam rubber or crumpled paper can be used to fill up partial rows of flips.

Small stacks of flips can be bound together for physical security using rubber bands. This is safe for only short time periods for a few days or less. The sulphur in the rubber bands can leach through the porous flip layer and produce a dark toned band across the coin's surface. This band may or may not be removed by using a silver dip. It is best to turn the top flip over so the paper card insert is between the rubber band and the coin. Long term storage of coins in flips should not be with rubber bands around or near the coins because of severe toning danger they cause.

Silver dollars have also been encapsulated in plastic holders that were sonically sealed. The coin could only be removed from these holders by cracking and breaking them apart.

The first plastic holders used to encapsulate silver dollars were those produced by the General Services Administration. They were relatively large in size and were sold by the GSA in 1972-74 and again in 1980. Almost three million uncirculated Carson City Morgan silver dollars were encapsulated in these holders. The plastic is inert and the coins are safe in these holders.

Paramount International Coin Corp. placed many of the Morgan and Peace silver dollars from the Redfield hoard in small sonically sealed plastic holders. These holders were the first to include the coin's grade and also identified that it was from the Redfield collection. They were marketed for three to five years beginning in 1976.

In 1986 the Professional Coin Grading Service began grading coins and placing them in sonically sealed plastic holders about the same size as the Paramount International Coin Corp. Redfield dollar holders. The card insert included the coin year and mint designation, overall grade number and coin identifying number. The encapsulated coin was safe in the inert plastic. Within a few years, several other coin grading services also encapsulated graded coins in similar size holders. Coins in the grading services holders are safe from handling and contamination dangers plus remain positively identified for each grading service's grade designation. However, the coins can not be handled separately for examination or photographing.

Albums

The earliest albums for displaying a silver dollar collection consisted of cardboard with cut-outs for the coin and the year and mint below this opening. A paper layer on the back of the board prevented the coin from falling out the rear but not the front. This type of coin album, while providing some measure of physical security because it held the coins separately, was very dangerous. The coin surfaces were exposed to the atmosphere. Further, the cardboard tended to tone the coin edges and the paper backing toned the coin reverses. Cardboard dust was present which could settle on the coin's surfaces. These inexpensive coin albums are not recommended for display of uncirculated silver dollars.

Later albums were somewhat improved by providing sliding windows of cellulose triacetate strips for the front and back of the coin openings in the board. This encapsulated the coin, better protecting it. The plastic in the windows was inert and clear to show the coin. However, the cardboard around the coin edges could still introduce some toning depending on how sulphur free the cardboard was and if cardboard dust would be present. But the new problem introduced by this type of album was the potential and real danger of the window slide edges scraping across the coin obverse high points as the slide was pushed into the page. This could cause fine parallel scratch lines in a horizontal direction in the hair and cheek area of the dollars. Albums with sliding windows are not recommended because of this danger.

For the past ten years or so, the all plastic album has been available. They were originally made of PVC plastic sheets with insert plastic holders, most also of PVC plastic. While they were clear and displayed the coins nicely with good physical security, they were extremely dangerous chemically. As with PVC flips, the plastic was unstable and generally broke down coating the coins, in some cases in less than a year. Later plastic album used an inert plastic holder to slide into a soft PVC plastic page. This at least eliminated the direct contact of the coin with the PVC plastic. But since the coins were still not in airtight holders, the PVC chemicals could still migrate to the coin surfaces. One safer alternative is to put each coin in a safe holder such as a "Kointain" that is airtight and then put them into the plastic album pages.

Albums made of three layers of plexiglas or lucite with cutouts in the center layer for the coins have been available since the 1960's. The three sections screwed together making a relatively airtight holder that displayed the coins in very clear and inert plastic. These albums are relatively expensive and bulky but provide excellent physical and chemical protection while displaying the coins nicely.

Recently available albums use chemically inert and airtight individual coin holders such as mylar, plexiglas or lucite. These are mounted in various ways in the page with some albums using pins to secure the holder, allowing it to be rotated so both coin sides can be viewed.

In evaluating individual holders and albums to house coins three factors need to be considered:

1. Material
2. Construction
3. Contamination of materials

The material immediately surrounding and in contact with the coin should be chemically stable and inert under normal storage conditions. Construction of the holder or album should protect the coin physically and be airtight. Contact should preferably be only on the coin edge or rim. If contact is made on the coin obverse or reverse surface, it should be with a relatively soft substance that will not abrade the surface. The coin should be held mechanically secure so it will not move around and it should not be exposed to sharp sliding edges. The holder or album should not be contaminated with potentially damaging paper dust or other foreign particles when it was manufactured or shipped.

GRADING EVOLUTION

Over the past years there has been much in the coin newspapers and journals on silver dollar grading. Grading has undergone a tremendous evolution in recent decades. This section will examine the Morgan and Peace silver dollar grading changes (and things unchanged) over the years, what makes a coin eye appealing, the condition availability and the effects of the grading evolution.

Early Development

Before the late 1960's the major grading concern was whether a coin was circulated or uncirculated. Rolls and bags of dollars were readily available from banks, Federal Reserve and the U.S. Treasury. Relatively few people collected or invested in these common coins. Then came the great silver dollar rush on the Treasury in 1964 when most of the remaining Morgan and Peace dollars were finally permanently released to the public. That meant the prices of these series would start the march upward.

Interest in these series increased with this sudden influx into the market of an attractive, large sized, silver coin. The standard grading reference used in the 1960's was Brown and Dunn. Coverage in circulated grades was fairly detailed but uncirculated was not described although several grades were mentioned in the introduction.

Still, knowledgeable dealers and collectors could tell some coins were more desirable and sold better than others. So, gradually in the late 60's and early 70's various terms evolved to describe uncirculated dollars. Most used terms such as BU, Choice, and Gem BU to describe increasingly desirable uncirculated coin grades and these were priced accordingly. The premium of a Gem coin usually was not that much over a BU or Choice. This was due to the large supply of rolls and bags for many dates.

But as the dollars were dispersed and the number of collectors and investors increased, supply and demand forced prices upward. Uncirculated grading terms became more and more complex. By the mid 70's well over 30 terms were routinely used to describe uncirculated dollars in the various publications. How was a collector/dealer/investor to know if BU Gem was any better than Choice Superb? Grading terminology was chaotic for uncirculated dollars.

Out of this confusion grew the ANA grading guide. When released in 1977, it recognized three levels of uncirculated or BU dollars with numerical grades based on the Sheldon numbering system. In practice this was reduced to MS60 and MS65 since MS70 was, in reality, nonexistent for dollars. Red book and other price guides plus many ads used these two MS grades in the late 1970's.

As the market prices for dollars continued to rise, the price differences between MS60 and MS65 became larger and larger in many instances. Actual pricing by many dealers and collectors developed to fall between and above these grades depending on how nice the coin's condition.

The 1980's

In October 1980, the *Coin Dealer Newsletter* (so called Grey Sheet) pricing guide added MS63 prices for dollars to reflect the widening gap of price between MS60 and MS65. The ANA grading guide added the intermediate grades of MS63 and MS67 in the Second Edition released late in 1981.

In March, 1985, the *Coin Dealer Newsletter* added the MS64 grade for silver dollars to fill the wide price gap that had developed between the MS63 and MS65 grades. By this time there were well over a dozen grading services following the pioneering of ANACS and INS in the mid-1970's. Collectors, investors and dealers actively traded certified graded coins by a number of these grading services. However, it was perceived that not all of the grading services used the same standards. There were also problems of self-serving interests when a grading service was also associated with a particular coin firm.

So, in the mid-1980's, grading was still chaotic and confusing for silver dollars. Many investors and collectors were being mislead and losing money when their certified graded coins didn't hold the value paid for them. Often coins certified by certain grading services were deeply discounted by dealers when buying them because the coins failed to meet their own grading standards. And there was confusion with the practices of split two-sided grading versus a single grade number.

To attempt to overcome these problems in coin grading, the Professional Coin Grading Service was formed in 1986. Coins graded by them were encapsulated in inert plastic with a label inside that specified the coin's overall grade and identification of date/mint. A group of dealers formed a trading network that would buy and sell PCGS graded coins on a sight unseen basis over electronic trading networks. The PCGS coin grading standards were adequately conservative so the coins traded at established price levels for the grades.

In a short time PCGS graded coins soon dominated the certified and graded coin market. Also, the perceived grading standards used by PCGS became the primary accepted one used by the coin industry. Most everyone began examining raw coins with the object of what grade would PCGS give it. Resubmittal of PCGS graded coins also became popular for those borderline graded coins with the hopes of achieving a higher grade. There were also perceived grading changes in PCGS graded coins over the years but these were small compared to the vast difference in grading standards used previously by the various grading services.

PCGS had introduced the eleven point grading for uncirculated coins in early 1986. The Third Edition of the ANA grading guide, released in 1987, added these eleven points and also utilized coin photographs rather than line drawings. The bid sheets summarizing the prices of the electronic trading network, American Numismatic Exchange, utilized these eleven point grade prices. These bid sheets soon became the dominant pricing guide for dealers as the encapsulated coins were traded similar to commodities. *The Certified Coin Dealer Newsletter* was added as a pricing guide using the eleven point grading. As could be expected, the coin prices became more volatile because of the instantaneous price reporting of the electronic trading network and the leverage that could be exercised by the market makers on these networks.

Other coin grading services soon followed the PCGS lead in encapsulating graded coins. But only a few grading services gained wide acceptance of their so-called slabbed coins – PCGS, NGC and ANACS. Grading standards were much more stable from 1986 onward than in the immediate previous years. But prices became the big variable instead, which is the way it should be in a free market economy.

Coin Grading Machines

The earliest claimed coin grading machine which the authors saw demonstrated was that of Dr. Sidney Auerback, in May 1985 at New York City. It had been demonstrated over the previous few years to several coin dealers. It consisted of a video camera, display terminal, analyzer and disc drive storage. Details revealed of the system were sketchy, but apparently it operated by integrating the light intensity in a horizontal line across the coin and displaying the horizontal line intensities as a profile with vertical distance. The machine could not provide a coin grade and was not very accurate in showing correlations among scanned coins and photos.

In August of 1986, the authors visited the Milton Roy Company in Rochester, NY, to view and participate in a coin grading machine demonstration by Henry Merton. Milton Roy Co. were leaders in image analysis. A demonstration using their Omnicon 3500 and its successor 1101 was made on coins. The system consisted of a high resolution video camera whose output went through shading correction, detection, digital analysis, storage and display. After some initial adjustments of the

machine through interactive tests of coin scanning by the authors, the machine demonstrated the capability to detect and display grading characteristics of abrasions, fullness of strike and loss of luster from wear. It could not at that time, provide a coin grading number. Henry Merton pursued the development of a grading machine and in February 1991, the announcement was made that a company he was associated with, CompuGrade, had starting grading coins using computer grading.

Meanwhile, in November 1986, Amos Press commissioned Battelle Memorial Institute of Columbus, Ohio, to determine the feasibility and practicality of using equipment to grade coins. By August 1987, Battelle reported that it was technically feasible to grade coins using various types of equipment such as laser scanning, optical scanning, high-resolution video imaging, holography and computerized image analysis. A working engineering model was subsequently developed which could demonstrate measuring various coin characteristics and computer software was worked on to analyze and display the measured data. In the summer of 1990, Amos Press bought the ANACS grading service of the ANA. The utilization of their computerized grading machine had not yet been announced by early 1992.

In May of 1990, after more than two years of development, PCGS demonstrated a coin grading machine called "PCGS Expert" and stated they had begun using it to grade coins. The "PCGS Expert" consisted of a single color video camera with sequenced lights around it. A stage automatically positioned the coins relative to the camera. Strike was measured on the obverse for Morgan dollars by counting the number of lines in the hair above the ear and on the reverse by the eagle's breast and claws. Luster was determined by measuring the amount of light scattered vertically from the coin to the camera from a low angle light. Abrasions were determined by sequencing lights to get various angle reflections. A marks analysis was performed for primary regions of interest which were the cheek, neck and left and right fields for the obverse. For these marks, histograms versus intensity were the basic analysis tool for comparisons of major characteristics. Then the characteristics of areas of interest were summed using various weighting factors to give the overall MS grade. This number could be modified considering the strength of strike, luster and eye appeal plus any minor characteristics.

Computer machine grading has thus arrived and promises to give consistent grading. However, the accuracy and consistency compared to traditional consensus grading by human graders depends a great deal on the parameters used to determine grades that are input to the machine and the various weighting factors that are used in analyzing the camera input data. Over a period of time, the grading machines will constantly be refined with improved accuracy and consistency. The number of coin series capable of being graded will be expanded from the initial ones of silver dollars. Ultimately the improved grading capabilities offered by computerized grading machines will lead to more consistent grading and to the betterment of the hobby.

GRADING FACTORS

Coin Value, that is what it is all about. A coin grade is translated into value by the collector/dealer/investor using various price grades. The grade in the coin examiner's mind may be a numerical one, descriptive term or just how nice the condition appears. The question is, what factors determine how nice a coin is (meaning value or price).

What makes a dollar eye appealing? It will of course depend upon the beholder (like beauty). But over the years five factors have become generally used:

1. Abrasion or wear
2. Strike
3. Luster
4. Color
5. Proof-like

Abrasions are scratches, scuff marks and contact marks in general on a coin's surface. Morgan and Peace dollars struck for circulation were all put into canvas bags of 1,000 coins by each mint. This was to facilitate the accounting and shipping of them. Transporting a bag of 1,000 dollars weighing 60 pounds caused abrasions on virtually every one of them. Of course fewer abrasions on a coin makes it more desirable. But the complication is what size, how many and where can these abrasions be to affect the coin's value. These are subjective judgments in many instances. Over the years, some accepted guidelines have evolved on these abrasions or bag marks. For the Morgan dollar the cheek area is the first, second and third most important area to look for these bag marks. It is a large raised area on the Liberty Head that was open and most vulnerable to abrasions. A relatively clean cheek is required for an eye appealing Morgan dollar but abrasions in other areas that are noticeable can also downgrade a coin. For the Peace dollar the cheek area is smaller but the Liberty Head neck and eagle's wing are more vulnerable to bag marks and thus important areas in grading.

Strike refers to the fullness of the design detail. Weak areas make the coin less attractive or valuable. For the Morgan dollar a weakness in strike typically shows up first in the hair above the Liberty Head ear and the eagle's breast feathers. For the Peace dollar it shows first in the hair over the Liberty Head ear and the eagle's wing feathers over the legs.

Luster refers to the frostiness of the design devices and the brilliance of the field. This is determined primarily by die wear. New dies used to strike coins will strike coins with frosty devices and brilliant fields. As the dies wear from striking thousands of coins, the frostiness is gradually polished away to give a more brilliant look and the fields become rough, producing a dull appearance. The coins are more attractive and valuable when there is frosting on the devices and brilliant fields producing a nice contrast. Luster of a coin can also be affected by coatings or contaminants on the surface.

Color is anything other than natural silver brilliance. It can be natural or artificial toning or dirt/grease coating. Natural toning occurs when silver oxidizes from being in contact or near canvas bags or paper with high sulfur content. It can be multicolored or a solid color and its attractiveness is very much a personal thing. Very dark tones or spotty toning is generally considered to be undesirable. Light dirt or grease coating picked up from many years storage in a bag does not affect the value but a heavy coating can decrease the value.

Proof-like refers to the degree of reflection in the coin's field. Basining of the Morgan dies to obtain a slight curvature for the field for better striking of the coins resulted in polished and smooth fields of the die. This in turn resulted in smooth mirror-like fields of the coins when they were struck. As the dies were used and wore, the field surface would become rough, gradually losing their reflective quality. Only the first five to ten thousand coins struck from a new Morgan die would result in proof-like (PL) coins unless it was again polished during its life to remove clash marks, for example. The greater the degree of reflectance, the more valuable the coin. A clear reflectance of at least three inches is required for a full PL and a deep mirror is one beyond about four to five inches. Both sides of a coin must be PL for a coin to be valued as a full PL. There are no PL Peace dollars because Peace dollar dies were not basined or polished except for some rare instances to repair a die that was badly clashed.

The most desirable and eye appealing coins with the highest value will therefore have a minimum of distracting bag marks, full strike with sharp detail, a cameo-type luster on the devices, with or without attractive toning and very deep mirrors. The state of these factors will determine the relative value of a coin.

CONDITION AVAILABILITY SPECTRUM

One of the most fascinating and frustrating things about Morgan and Peace dollars is the fact that the dates and mints are not equally available with the same eye appealing factors of abrasions, strike, luster, color, and proof-like. There can be no such thing as a matched series of Morgan or Peace dollars. Differences in the basining of the dies, planchet preparation, striking of the coins, coin storage and transportation, and the survival percentage preclude identical looking coins for all dates and mints.

For mint state coins there can be approximated curves of the relative number of surviving coins within the various coinages of the five grading factors.

For example, under abrasions, years like 81-S or 03-P tend to have a higher percentage of coins available with a minimum of bag marks as compared to a 78-CC or 95-S which tend to be bag marked or "baggy" as they say. This can be illustrated in a chart in *Figure 17-1* which shows the degree of abrasions on a horizontal axis versus the relative surviving number in mint state on a vertical axis.

The distribution of abrasions for other dates and mint would have curves somewhere between these two extremes. When translated into a grade number, this same chart shown in *Figure 17-2* would show a higher proportion of coins falling into the MS65 range for the 81-S and the 03-P than the 78-CC or 95-S. Note that, within say, the MS65 grade, there is a definite range of surviving number of coins from slightly better than average number of abrasions to a number approaching the minimum number of abrasions. This shows that even within a grade number "some are better than others." There will be some MS65 coins just approaching the minimum number of abrasions for MS67 and others that have a number of approaching that for MS63. In other words, the continuous distribution curve for MS63, 65 and 67 results in ranges for each grade and not just a single point on the distribution curve.

Similar curves of the relative number of surviving mint state can also be shown for strike as illustrated in *Figure 17-3*. Again, certain dates will show distribution curves skewed at one extreme or the other such as the 81 S which normally are fully struck and 02-O which are normally slightly weakly struck. These differences were caused by the different die basining and strike pressures used by the various mints.

A chart illustrating the variances in luster is shown in *Figure 17-4*. In this case, the later P mints of 1901 to 1904 tend to mostly have brilliant surfaces on the devices while some years like the 80-S have a fairly high percentage of coins with significant frosting. These differences were caused by the state of frostiness of the master hub and dies in use at the time, the number of coins struck while the die was in service, and the manufacturing process used at each mint for the planchets.

Proof-likes can also be charted to show the relative surviving number in mint state as shown in *Figure 17-5*. Certain Morgan dollar dates like the 81-S have a high percentage of PL and DMPL coins while others like an 01-P are extremely scarce in PL. This was due to the length of service of the dies which tended to be longer in later years of the Morgan series and the coin melts in 1917 and 1918 which destroyed about half of the Morgan dollars minted.

MINT STATE GRADING CHANGE EFFECTS

Back in the late 1970's when there were but two practical MS grades of MS60 and MS65, they each covered a wide spectrum of the MS coin condition. This is illustrated in *Figure 17-6*. Some dates like the 81-S had a fairly high proportion of MS65 coins in comparison to others such as the 80-O which had a relatively small proportion in that grade. But many MS65's were better or lower than the average because of the wide grade spectrum.

Then in October 1980 the addition of MS63 to the Grey Sheet pricing guide changed the coverage of MS60 and MS65. MS67 was also added but not listed in the Grey Sheet because of the limited availability and market for that grade. The addition of these two grades narrowed the surviving spectrum average for MS60 and MS65 as shown in *Figure 17-7*.

That is, the better MS65's prior to October 1980 became MS67's and the lower MS65's became part of the MS63 spectrum. Also the better MS60's became part of the new MS63 grade. This is illustrated in *Figure 17-8*.

The shaded area shows the grading spectrums absorbed from the old MS60 and MS65 into the new MS63 and MS67 grades. This had the effect of tightening up the MS65 grading spectrum with the more baggy or weakly struck old MS65 becoming MS63. So the MS65 grade encompassed fewer coins of the MS spectrum and they tended to be of better average condition. That is because coins that became MS67 were much fewer than those that became MS63.

Those people who bought coins with a condition at the lower end of the old MS65 spectrum but at full MS65 price suddenly found that their MS65 coins had changed to MS63 grade and price with a loss in value. But, if they had paid a price below the standard MS65 price, then the true value of the coin probably had not changed much even though the grade fell from the low end of the old MS65 to the upper part of the new MS63 spectrum.

Another effect on the coin grading and value is the condition of the coin market. In a rising or hot market, demand is ahead of the supply and the full spectrum of coins in say, the MS65 grade can be bought and sold. In a slow or receding market the supply outstrips the demand. This has the effect of the buyer demanding the upper part of the spectrum of a grade and a general tightening of grading for coins traded.

So, during 1980 through 1982 there were two effects of the tightening of the MS65 grading; the narrowing of the MS65 condition spectrum range with the addition of MS63 and MS67, and the slow market where buyers demanded the better coins within a grade range. This was the result of the grading evolution process and not a grading revolution.

The addition of the MS64 grade in March 1965 and the eleven point grading early in 1986 further narrowed the spread of each grade. Dominance of encapsulated graded coins after their introduction by PCGS early in 1986 established a coin grade, except by resubmittal. In a slow market, such as 1990-1991, the buyers could still be choosy and pick out the upper end coins in a particular grade.

But why do we need all of the MS grades and their complexity? Can a MS65 coin be accurately graded

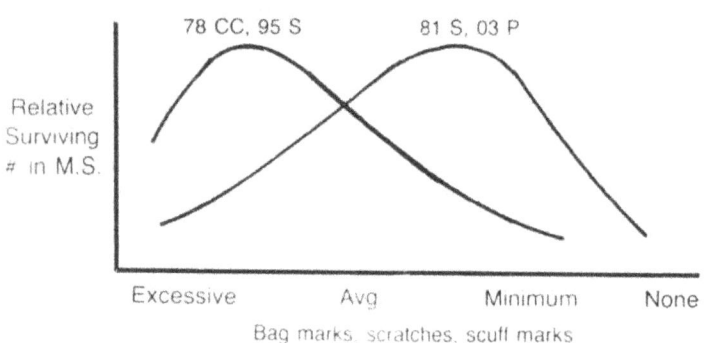

Figure 17-1 **ABRASIONS DISTRIBUTION**

Relative Surviving # in M.S.

78 CC, 95 S   81 S, 03 P

Excessive   Avg   Minimum   None

Bag marks, scratches, scuff marks

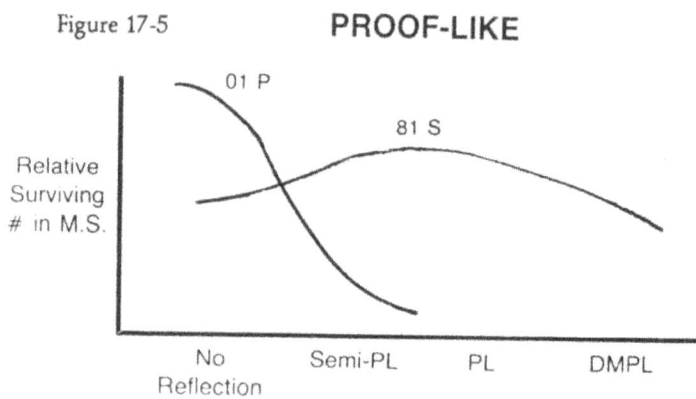

Figure 17-5 **PROOF-LIKE**

Relative Surviving # in M.S.

01 P   81 S

No Reflection   Semi-PL   PL   DMPL

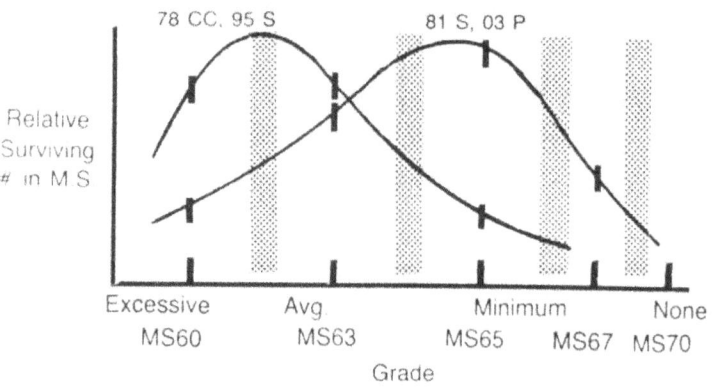

Figure 17-2

ABRASIONS DISTRIBUTIONS WITH GRADE

Relative Surviving # in M.S.

78 CC, 95 S   81 S, 03 P

Excessive MS60   Avg. MS63   Minimum MS65   None MS67 MS70

Grade

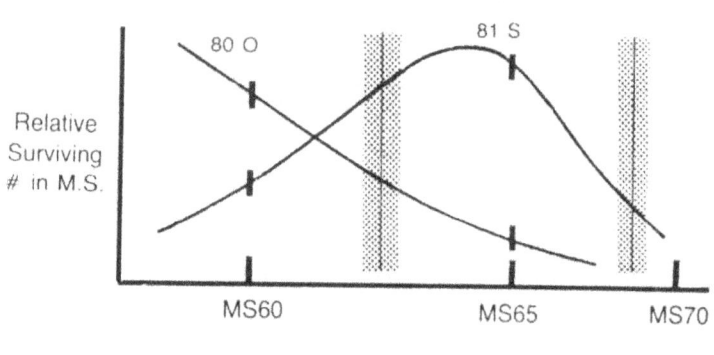

Figure 17-6

THREE MS GRADE DISTRIBUTIONS

Relative Surviving # in M.S.

80 O   81 S

MS60   MS65   MS70

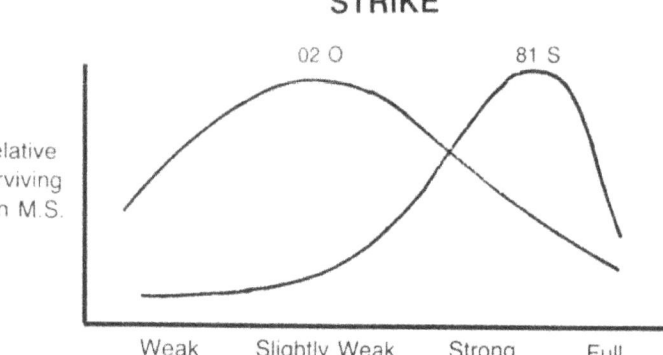

Figure 17-3 **STRIKE**

Relative Surviving # in M.S.

02 O   81 S

Weak   Slightly Weak   Strong   Full

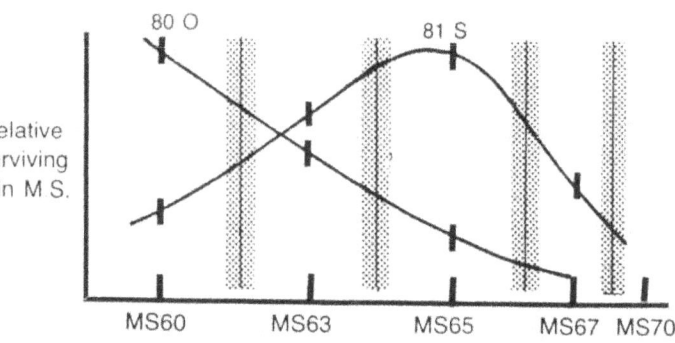

Figure 17-7 **FIVE MS GRADE DISTRIBUTIONS**

Relative Surviving # in M.S.

80 O   81 S

MS60   MS63   MS65   MS67 MS70

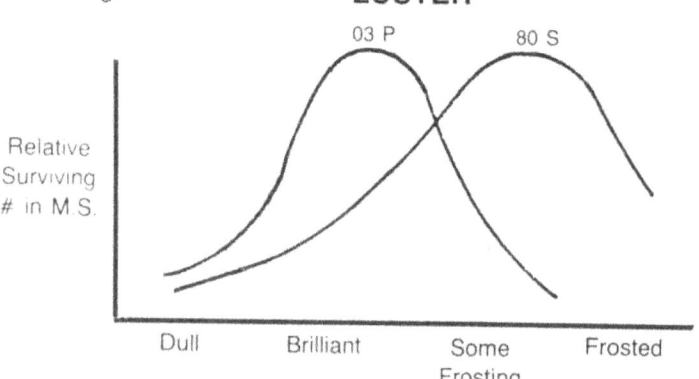

Figure 17-4 **LUSTER**

Relative Surviving # in M.S.

03 P   80 S

Dull   Brilliant   Some Frosting   Frosted

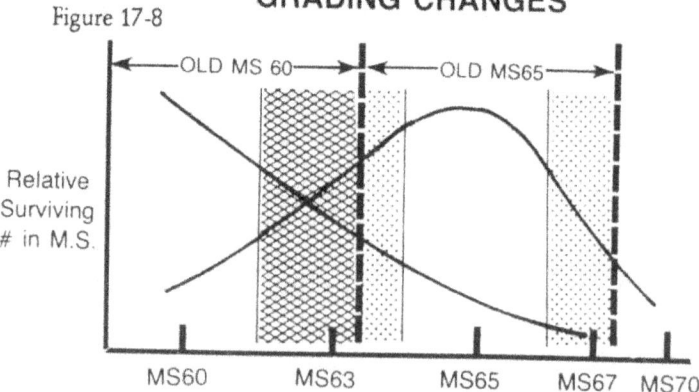

GRADING CHANGES

Figure 17-8

Relative Surviving # in M.S.

OLD MS 60   OLD MS65

MS60   MS63   MS65   MS67   MS70

and differentiated from a MS64? Yes – but only with experience. It is the areas of the condition spectrum where one grade merges into another such as MS64 merges into MS63 and MS64 into MS65 that is the hardest to grade. Valuewise it is probably easier to get some agreement. But to assign a specific grading number is still, after all, an opinion with much subjective input. The idealized grading areas with a fine line dividing as shown in the charts in reality become grading areas with overlaps and wide dividing bars because of differing opinions.

GRADING SCALE

A grading scale describes the various conditions of a coin in uncirculated and circulated condition. This scale can be one using adjectives or numbers. Up until the late 1970's, adjectives were used exclusively to denote the condition grade of silver dollars. These adjectives were fairly well standardized for the circulated grades. The uncirculated grades generally used BU, Choice and Gem to denote the increasingly higher uncirculated grades. But many other adjectives were also used for uncirculated silver dollars such as select and superb, plus their various combinations.

With the publishing of the ANA grading guide in 1977 a numerical scale as well as adjectives was introduced for grading silver dollars. It was based on the scale used in Dr. William Sheldon's book, *Penny Whimsy*. This was a scale from 1 to 70 and originally reflected the change of value with condition for large cents. The coin market has since changed to make the Sheldon scale inaccurate for determining the value of large cents for each condition. But the Sheldon scale gained popularity and was adapted for indicating the grading condition for other series. Incorporation into the ANA grading guide for all U.S. series gave the Sheldon grading scale a basis for widespread use.

The current most popular U.S. coin pricing guide, the *Coin Dealer Newsletter* or "Grey Sheet," uses adjectives to describe circulated grades and Sheldon numbers for the uncirculated or mint state grades. In addition, most collectors, dealers, and investors use adjectives to refer to circulated grades and in the uncirculated grade designations, the Sheldon numbers in eleven points from MS60 to MS70. A few still use the old adjectives of Typical, Select, Choice and Gem and others use the older terms of Choice, Gem and Superb Gem or a host of other terms to designate uncirculated grades. The authors support the ANA grading guide and numerical scale designations because it is the most widely used grading reference.

The quantitative grading numbers of the ANA grading guide range from 1 which is the basal state of a barely recognizable silver dollar to mint state 70 for a coin in perfect state, just as it left the dies. Silver dollars below condition 7, very good, are not generally collectable except for the rarest years and mints. Business strikes do not exist in MS70 since they were all placed in bags of 1,000 coins for transportation where they picked up abrasions.

The following sections discuss and illustrate the coin examination procedures and the various grading factors of abrasions/wear, strike, luster, color and proof-like.

EXAMINING SILVER DOLLARS

Collectors, dealers and investors of Morgan and Peace silver dollars will need to examine them for two reasons: (1) to determine their grade and thus value, and (2) to identify error coins or die varieties. The first reason is by far the most frequent need for most people.

Grading Examination

The grading of silver dollars requires experience, experience and more experience! There are many factors in grading dollars as discussed later in this chapter. This section will briefly examined some of the techniques and mechanics of examining and grading coins.

First, there must be adequate lighting to examine the coin's surface. Most dealers at coin shows and coin stores have moveable incandescent lamps. It is best to be within several feet of the lamp to obtain bright enough light. Overhead lighting at coin shows and in coin stores may not be bright or numerous enough to provide sufficient lighting on the coin. Also, the type of lighting may be different than normal. This can cause an emphasis on the frosted device. For example, the cameo proof-like (PL) you bought at a show may be just a nice frosted coin when re-examined at home under more usual lighting! Or worse yet, hairline scratches or scuff marks may suddenly appear later under better light and you then get a sinking feeling of having overpaid for the coin.

Lighting for grading at your normal working area, whether at home or at the office, should be from a desk lamp. It can be either a fixed or movable incandescent lamp. Fluorescent type lights should be avoided because they are too long and the light is too diffused to detect hairlines. Personal preference and space will dictate the type. All that is required is that the incandescent lamp provide relatively close and bright enough light. A small spot of light such as that provided by Tensor-type lights is generally not recommended since a point source of light will cause too many bright and dark spots on the coin's surface. But these are suited for detecting hairlines.

It is best to examine the coins out of a holder. This may not always be possible if the coin is in a sealed, encapsulated, stapled or screw holder. The plastic film of the flip or cardboard holder should be clear enough so it does not mask, cloud or distort the appearance of the coin's surface. If in doubt about some part or feature of a coin, ask the dealer or person for permission **first** before removing the coin from a holder. It is only common courtesy. The coin was put in a holder for protection. Most owner's of coins will provide a tray or cloth so the coins can be removed from the holder and placed on a soft surface for examination without dropping it on a hard surface. You would not want to be embarrassed and have to buy a coin you dropped on the floor or case. A silver dollar dropped at a coin show causes considerable noise and undesirable attention!

Always handle a coin by the **edges**. When passing a coin to another person be sure they have a tight grip on the edge before you release your grip. As a precaution, place your free hand under the coin when passing it as this is the most likely time a coin could be accidentally dropped.

Most of the time, examination of silver dollars can be satisfactorily performed in currently available flips. Searching through a double row box of coins can be done without taking each holder out of the box. Simply make sure there is enough room in the row to flip the coins toward you so you can see the obverse clearly. This may require that some holders be temporarily removed from the back of the row to give adequate room. In this way the date, mint and condition of interest can be spotted while flipping through the holders in a box.

When a coin of interest is found you should take the holder out of the box and examine both obverse and reverse. Look first for any signs of wear to see if the coin is circulated or uncirculated. Be careful of AU and sliders as they can be deceptive! Tilt the coin to see if there are any grey areas on the high points of the design or in the field that indicate wear.

Grading a circulated coin is a matter of determining the degree of wear as specified hereafter. Grading an uncirculated coin requires consideration of bag marks, strike, luster, color, proof-like and overall eye appeal. This is more complex and requires practice and experience.

It usually helps if the coin is held of to the side so that the light is not directly reflected in a straight line from the coin to your eye. The bag marks and scratches will show up better with this side lighting on the coin surface. **Tilt** the coin back and forth to get optimum lighting to show up these bag marks and scratches. With a little practice, this technique will become second nature.

Most people can grade dollars with the naked eye. Others use a variety of magnifying glasses to show up the nicks, scratches or strength of strike. These can be 3x wide angle glass with or without a built-in light. Others use a 7x or 10x glass to examine clearly the coin detail. It all depends on how good your eyes are, experience and what you are used to.

It is difficult to detect hairline polishing, faint scuff marks or a fine scratch with just the naked eye. Tilt the coin carefully at various angles to the light to catch any of these defects on a coin's surface. A magnifying glass may be required to really confirm their presence.

Be particularly wary of toned coins! They may be hiding these defects or a weak strike. Look through the toning at the coin's surface to detect bag marks, hairlines and scratches. Unfortunately, coins may be artifi-

cially toned to hide surface defects. It is best to stay clear of toned coins until experience in grading brilliant coins is obtained or they are purchased from a reliable dealer/collector.

When examining loose coins from a roll be careful to not let the coins slide against one another. The roll owner will not appreciate you adding more marks to the coins! Either place the stack of coins on a stable surface and examine them one by one or hold the roll securely in one hand and remove single pieces or groups of coins carefully with the other hand. Do not let the coins bang against one another or drop them!

Variety Examination

The large size of the silver dollar makes it relatively easier to examine than the smaller denomination coins for several reasons: (1) they are easier to handle, (2) the design, lettering, date, and mint marks are considerably larger, and (3) any variations in design are more evident, sometimes even to the naked eye.

Another important factor is that a great many of the available coins in this series are either in uncirculated condition or at least in a high grade which makes for easier examination.

On the other hand, being larger in size, they have more area to examine and the serious collector will want to look for doubling and other details even more carefully than on other denomination of coins. The use of a good magnifying glass or stereo microscope is highly recommended for a comprehensive study of this series.

A comfortable straight backed chair and a flat top with ample working space make long sessions of examining coins easier and more efficient. A cloth or paper placed on top of the table will protect the uncirculated coins and also protect the table top from dirty circulated coins.

Before examining circulated or badly tarnished uncirculated coins, they may have to be selectively cleaned using the procedures outlined in the chapter on silver dollar preservation and storage. It can be very frustrating trying to decide if the material around the date or mint mark is due to doubling or just dirt. Excessively dirty coins can have much of the fine coin detail hidden while heavily tarnished coins often have poor surface contrast which makes it difficult to discern specific coin details.

Lighting

Proper lighting is also very important in order to be able to examine small variety details of a coin. Incandescent table lamps, and small high intensity lamps are all satisfactory and the choice depends on one's personal preference and what is available. The important thing is to have the working area well lighted and to adjust the lamp so it does not present any glare.

Lighting at coin shows can be variable – from excellent to practically nonexistent. More than one collector (or cherry picker) has thought they had found a nice variety at a show only to have it somehow disappear when reexamined at home. Most of the time this is due to poor lighting.

The standard lighting at a coin show is movable incandescent light. But you need to get at least within a few feet of the light to clearly see the minor varieties. Some dealers may not have lights at their tables. In such a case, ask the dealer if you can examine the coin at a nearby table that has proper lighting. Most ceiling lights at coin shows do not provide adequate lighting for close examination of coins.

At home you should have either a movable or fixed incandescent desk lamp. You cannot rely on overhead or floor lamps to provide enough light for close up studying of coins. The Tensor type lights should be avoided as too much of a point source of light will cause a mixture of bright and dark spots on the coin. The movable feature of the lamp allows the light to be moved to the best position while remaining comfortably seated and not bending over or causing back strain.

When examining a coin, it should be tilted and rotated in relation to the light to bring out the desired detail. Low angle viewing is also very often effective.

Magnifying Glass

Magnifying glasses are required in most cases for examining the coin detail to identify die varieties. Most of the planchet and striking errors can be identified with the naked eye although one may want to examine some of the finer detail with a lens to confirm the cause or to detect counterfeits. Shown in the photograph are some typical hand held lens and choices of wide and narrow fields in these lens are generally available. The more expensive lens usually have less distortion at the field edges and coated glass for better light transmission.

The 7 to 10x hand held magnifying glass are the most useful in identifying varieties. The 7x can aid in determining the more prominent varieties but 10x is needed on some of the more minor doubling. 16x is used by some collectors for detailed study. Most of the time and for most general use, the 10x glass is more than sufficient.

As in most things, there are various quality magnifying glasses. A single lens is useful up to about 3x. To study varieties at least a doublet is required which is a glass with two lens. Cost for these is relatively inexpensive, generally in the ten dollar or less range. Such double lens glass are available up to about 16x. The two lens, except in the more expensive types, cannot correct distortion at the edge of the field. This effectively narrows the

usable field down. It also puts added strain on the eyes due to the distortion. Some people get use to the doublets and have used them for many years.

The best hand held glasses are the Hastings Triplet design type. With three lens, the field can be distortion free from edge to edge. If you ever start using a Triplet type glass you will never want to revert back to the doublet type. The coin detail will be much clearer with little distortion once things are in focus. A 10x Triplet is sufficient to pick out most varieties and identify them.

The main disadvantage of Triplet glasses is their price. Generally, they cost $20-30. But if you really want to study the coins the price is well worth it in the saved time and eye strain. Various brands are available but Bausch and Lomb is very popular. A wide range of powers can be had from 3 to 25x. Just do not forget and leave them behind on the table at shows!

Stereo Microscope

A stereo microscope is best for showing detail clearly and at high power. However, it has some disadvantages being bulky in even the smallest models, making them difficult to bring and use at coin shows. Only die hards are seen using stereo microscopes at coin shows! These instruments are best used at home.

It also takes some time to place the coin under the microscope and to adjust the lighting and focus. A hand held magnifying glass is usually much quicker for examination unless one is systematically examining a large number of coins for varieties. Focusing and tilting the coin for best lighting effect soon becomes second nature and takes just a few seconds.

The stereo microscope should generally be reserved for examining those coins that are more difficult to VAM because of weaker detail needing higher magnification of 20 to 60x. It is also useful to blow up the coin detail if unusual doubling, die breaks or design needs to be checked and a hand held glass just does not provide the clarity

Hand-Held Lenses

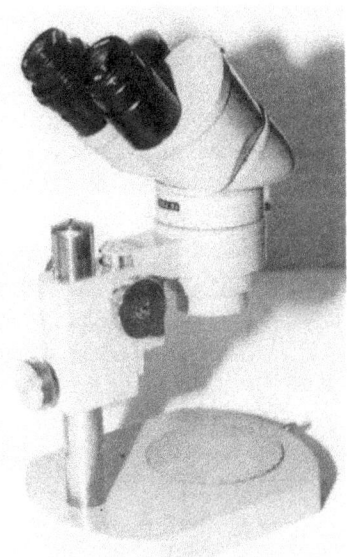

Stereo Microscope

needed.

There are many stereo microscopes an the market. The photograph shows a quality instrument. Cost of such an instrument is about $300 or greater to get quality optics. Lower priced instruments will have greater distortion - particularly in the edge of the field and dimmer edges. This will make it more difficult to focus and will tire the eyes more quickly. Stage illumination is not necessary since the spot lights provided are poor for coin lighting. They cause too many bright spots and dark areas. A broader lamp that is adjustable and provides a more diffuse light is better. One or more Tensor type lamps usually will work well.

You may also want to consider getting a camera attachment for one of the eyepieces. Excellent pictures can be obtained using a 35 mm SLR. At least make sure that the adapter is available for the microscope if you have any photographic inclination and might decide to pursue it in the future.

It is also very handy to have a turret on the microscope to change magnification powers quickly. With this feature you can quickly switch from 20x to 40 or 60x to double check a feature. Otherwise you will need to switch eyepieces (or objective lens which is even harder).

The 15x to 45x is the most useful magnifying range and a wide field of view is recommended. Sloping eyepieces make viewing coins somewhat easier but this feature is not necessary. For the serious variety collector, the stereo microscope will soon pay for itself many times over both in the ease of examining coins and in the greater accuracy made possible in studying the coin's detail.

Identifying Varieties

78-P - Starting with the date with the largest number of die varieties, here the key is the reverse, to quickly narrow down the possibilities. First, determine which of the four basic reverse types the coin has - 8 TF, 7/8 TF, 7 TF PAF or 7 TF SAF. These are easily identified and a magnifying glass is not needed except for the weaker 7/8 TF varieties. The next step is to identify the sub-type of the reverse - the A^1 or A^2/A^1 8 TF, the particular 7/8 TF die variety, the B^1 or B^2 7 TF PAF, and the C^1, C^2 or C^3 7 TF SAF. From this point, several different paths can be taken depending upon one's preference and experience.

For the 8 TF, check with a magnifying glass the added feathers between the eagle's wings and legs against the VAM book photographs. Each A^1 die was touched up in this area and the added feathers are unique. The A^2/A^1 dies have unique doubling on the eagle's beak which is fairly easy to identify for a specific die variety. Some 8 TF reverse dies were with a number of obverse dies. These can be narrowed down by checking the specific doubled obverse areas against the VAM book photos and descriptions. With experience and

study, certain doubled areas can be used as diagnostic for a given die variety. Some collectors even make detailed reference notes on obverse and reverse coin outline drawings of the key doubled areas.

7/8 TF dies are fairly easy to identify by determining the number of tail feather ends showing and comparing them with the book photos. Of course, the VAM 44 is easy to spot (but hard to find) by the unique doubling of the cotton bolls and leaves of the obverse.

The 7 TF PAF varieties are the hardest to identify of the 78-P series because there are so many die varieties and many are very similar. First, narrow down the sub type of the reverse, i.e., B^1a, B^1b, B^2a, B^2b, etc. Then, check the obverse to see if it is of the II/I type. If it is, then look at LIBERTY or other doubled features and compare with book photographs. Some II/I and II varieties are very close and require careful comparison of book description and coin features. Other varieties have distinctive features such as a tripled star or broken letters which allow for quick identification.

Narrowing down the C reverse varieties is a similar process as the B reverses. After the reverse sub type is identified, then check the obverse for II/I, II, or III specific varieties.

78-S - This date has many different doubled date and design varieties. The B^1 (long center arrow shaft) variety is of course easy to identify, but much scarcer than the B^2 (short center arrow shaft) variety. The hard part is to identify the engraved wing feather varieties. These have a re-engraved feather between the eagle's right wing and leg which are very similar looking. It requires careful study of the bottom curvature of this feather and other details to identify the specific variety out of about 25 known. The 79-S also has this engraved feather variety but fewer in number (about 10).

Overdates and Over Mint Mark - The two years of overdates (1880, 1887) and over mint marks (1882, 1900) are for the most part easily identifiable varieties. The major 80-P overdates (VAM's 6-9) are each very distinctive. The minor 80-P overdates with 8/7 checkmark can be distinguished by other doubling of the date.

80-CC overdates are easy to identify by the strong 80/79 and 8/7 varieties or the reverse type of the 8/7 dash varieties.

80-O overdates VAM's 4,5, and 6 are easily distinguishable. The VAM 6, 6A, and 6B can be identified by the reverse die gouge in left wreath or hangnail eagle. The VAM's checkmark can be identified by doubling of the date or reverse mint mark.

80-S overdates are also easily distinguishable using the book photographs. The 87-P and 87-O 7/6 overdates are no problem with but one overdate each.

82-O -O/S over mint mark VAM's 3,4 and 5 are easy to tell apart. The various die states require careful examination with a 10x glass to separate one from another.

00-O -O/CC VAM's 7-12 are fairly easy to identify using the VAM book photographs. Do not confuse VAM 7 with VAM 9 (detached short right loop of C).

2 Olive Reverse - These are dual hub C^4/C^3 varieties which occur on the 00-P, 01-P, 01-O, 01-S, 02-P, 02-O, 02-S, 03-S and 04-S. Unless the variety has some unique doubled date, ear or mint mark feature, these are very difficult to distinguish apart. The 01-O has over ten and the 02-O has over seventeen, 2 olive reverses making them a real challenge to identify. The doubled features are similar for all these varieties and sometimes they can be best resolved by die polishing lines next to the eagle's legs or mint mark position.

Other - Most of the other dates have only doubled dates and mint marks with an occasional doubled die feature elsewhere on the coin. Minor doubled dates and mint mark and their combinations can be a bear to identify. It is not unusual to get stuck on some of these minor varieties and take 20-30 minutes tracing one down. This is particularly true of 80-S, 82-S and other dates with a large number of varieties. It requires careful study of the doubling of each date digit and mint mark doubling plus the combination of obverse and reverse dies to finally pin down a particular minor variety.

One should start with a quick examination of the date and mint mark to see if they have any unique doubling features. For the S and O mints, it is sometimes easier to determine the particular mint mark doubling variety and then narrow down the obverse combinations.

ABRASION/WEAR

Abrasions are one of the major factors in determining the grade of a mint state of an uncirculated silver dollar. Wear is the grading criteria for circulated silver dollars and is described and illustrated in later sections for the Morgan and Peace dollars.

Abrasions can take many forms on a dollar. The most common are the so-called **bag marks**. These are surface indentations, scuff areas, scratches, and scrapes caused by the dollars coming in contact with one another during the minting process, counting, bagging and transportation. Immediately after the striking of the silver dollar in the minting press, the lower die rose to push the coin up out of the collar. Then the press feed fingers pushed the coin off the lower die back towards the rear of the press into a chute where the coin dropped into a collection box. Naturally coins dropping on top of one another caused contact marks. Next, the full box of Morgan dollars was taken to the reviewing room to be inspected for flaws and counted. The Morgan dollars were dumped onto tables where more abrasions were imparted. After counting, the dollars were dropped into canvas bags of 1,000 coins again causing more marks. For the Peace dollar, the box of coins from the presses were dumped into bins and run through counting machines where they dropped into the canvas bags of 1,000 coins collecting many abrasions in this process.

Typical Scrapes of MS60

All business strike Morgan and Peace silver dollars ended up in canvas bags of 1,000 coins. This was the standard shipping and value container. They were sealed at the mint with a weight tolerance of two hundredths of an ounce total. Thereafter the bag of coins was carried, thrown, and dropped from place to place and transported via stagecoach, wagon, railroad car, boat, automobile and truck to various bank destinations. During this process, the coins shifted and jostled within the bag picking up more bag marks. Their large size and the nearly 60 pounds weight of a bag caused many marks on most silver dollars even though they may never have been placed into circulation. Not all bags were subjected to the same movements, so abrasions on the coins in bags will vary among bags of a given date and among those from various mints and years. And within a given bag, coins will exhibit a full spectrum of bag marks from minimum to excessive.

The placement and extent of a bag mark on the coin will affect how attractive the coin is and therefore its grade and value. The first place most people notice and examine on a silver dollar is the large open cheek area. A bag mark in the center of the cheek will be more noticeable than one in the hair or side of the field. Also, a light scuff or frost break is less noticeable than a deep cut or scrape. The extent and placement of bag marks for the various MS grades is illustrated and described in a later section. Large scrapes, typical of a MS60 coins are shown in the accompanying photograph.

Rim Dents and nicks are another form of abrasions. Rim nicks are a form of bag marks and are caused by coins contacting one another in uncirculated grade. In circulated grade the rim nicks are caused by the coin contacting various surfaces. A rim dent is a flattened area on the edge of the coin usually caused by dropping the coin on a hard floor. Large and noticeable rim dents can lower the grade of a coin one full grade step.

Hairlines are another form of abrasions and are fine parallel lines scratched into the coin's surface. They are generally caused when the coin was accidentally or intentionally brushed against cloth or other similar object. Some well meaning non-numismatists will use a cloth to rub a coin to remove dirt or toning to give a coin a shiny "new" look. Unfortunately, the cloth texture causes hairline scratches on both uncirculated and circulated coins.

Rim Dent

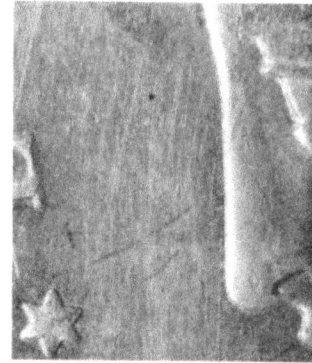

1921-S Hairlines in FIeld

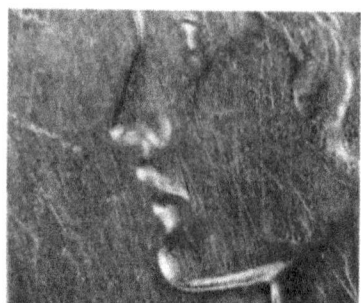

1928-P Slider AU Hairlines

Polished Coin

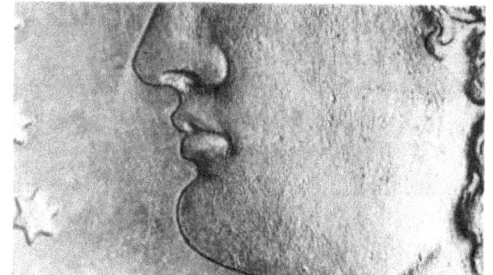

Whizzed Coin

Sometimes the hairlines will show up only on the front of the cheek or on areas of the field. Hairlines can be detected by tilting the coin under a strong light or using a 3 to 7 power magnifying glass. A couple of light hairlines will generally not lower a coin's grade. But large spots or areas can lower it one grade point. If the hairlines are extensive over the whole coin's surface, the grade may be reduced to AU. See the accompanying photographs of hairlines in the field of a 1921-S which lowers the grade one point and also a photograph of a 1928-P with extensive hairlines grading as a slider AU.

A **polished** coin is somewhat related to hairlines, except the rubbing is more severe on the coin's surface. Repeated rubbing of the surface will remove the coin's luster producing an overall shiny appearance with rounded edges of the design detail. Silver polish has also been used on silver dollars producing an even, shiny, polished look. The extreme is a whizzed coin which has been held against a buffing wheel. This buffing wheel may be cloth with polish or a fine wire wheel. The latter produces many fine scratches all over the surface giving an unnatural satiny appearance. Such severely polished or whizzed coins generally reduce their value to below that of EF or to junk uncollectible coins. Both uncirculated and circulated coins should never be subjected to polishing of any sort as it disturbs the luster of an uncirculated coin and creates an unnatural shiny look to even a circulated coin. The accompanying photograph shows an example of a polished coin. The most heartbreaking

example of a polished coin that the author's have seen is the first Morgan dollar struck, the Hayes' specimen which has unfortunately been polished repeatedly over the years giving this unique proof dollar a shiny polished look.

STRIKE

Missing design detail on a coin is usually due to a weak strike. Insufficient striking pressure will cause some areas of a planchet not being forced into contact with all parts of the die design cavities. This results in some of the design detail missing on the coin and parts of the design with lower than normal relief. Usually the missing and flat design is at the deepest part of the large die cavities - the center of the Liberty Head or eagle. Sometimes the peripheral lettering and stars will show weaknesses from insufficient striking pressure. A coin with missing detail is not as attractive and is worth less in value.

Striking of silver dollars was under the control of the die setters and press operators at each of the mints. The die setters would install and align the dies and then adjust the **striking pressure** to bring up the proper detail on the struck coins. The press operator, supervisors and inspectors would examine the coins during production to detect any striking defects. If any defects were noted, then the die setter was called in to adjust the press operation. Striking pressure was a compromise between using a high enough pressure to bring out all of the design detail but low enough to not get excessive finning or metal flow between the dies and collars at the rim. Also, the lower the striking pressure the less wear and strain on the dies so they could strike more coins per die pair before they wore out. Each mint and die setter established their own standards of compromise in striking pressure between adequate design detail on the coins and die service life.

Certain dates and mints are notorious for having produced coins from weak strikes. The New Orleans Mint struck many dates showing weak strikes such as 1883-1885, 1887-1897 and 1904. But not all coins of these years show weak strikes. On the other hand, the Philadelphia Mint generally produced well struck coins. But occasionally some Philadelphia Mint coins will be weakly struck such as 1888, 1921 and 1922. The San Francisco Mint produced many years with fully struck coins. But also some S mint show weak strikes for 1894, 1921, 1922, 1923, 1925, and 1928 years. The Carson City Mint was also not immune to producing weak strikes which occurred in 1885 and 1892. Virtually every year and mint will have at least a few weakly struck coins. Conversely, years and dates notorious for weak strikes will have some fully struck coins.

For the Morgan dollar, another variable was present that affected the strength of the strike at each mint. Pre-1921 Morgan dies were all individually **basined** at each mint. This gave a clear definition between the devices and field and produced a radius of curvature of the field so the design would be optimally brought up all over the coin surface with a minimum of striking pressure. Each mint used a revolving disk with polishing compound to polish the field to a given radius. Tolerances in the disk surfaces, its wear, and the care of the workman resulted in differences in the field radius of curvature of the dies at each mint and from year to year. Dies not optimally basined combined with inadequate striking pressure resulted in inadequately struck coins. This explains why the New Orleans Mint produced many weakly struck coins - it was from improperly basined dies. It also explains why some coins have less rim detail then others since the field radius of curvature determines whether the metal flows evenly across the coin or whether it flows more to the central devices or to the rim.

Dies also sank sometimes during use. The high striking pressures occasionally caused the surface of the die to distort and become uneven resulting in coins with wavy fields.

Some examples of weakly struck Morgan dollar obverses are shown in the accompanying photographs. A slightly weak strike will show a few hair strands missing just above the ear. This would not lower the value or grade of an otherwise MS63 or MS65 coin, but would be unacceptable for a MS66 coin. Obvious flatness of the hair above the ear and some flatness in the ear detail would be unacceptable for MS65 grades. Coins showing some weakness in the peripheral lettering, outer design

details, and denticles did not happen as often as weak central detail and does not affect the grade as much.

Also shown are some examples of weakly struck Morgan dollar reverses. A slightly weak struck reverse will lack clear definition of the central breast feathers of the eagle. Obvious weakness on the leg feathers and talons would be unacceptable for an MS65 coin. Extremely weak strikes will show flat areas on the wing feathers, arrow shafts and feathers, and the eagle's claws. Some of the New Orleans Mint dollars with weak strikes show a dimple or depression in the lower breast area which is called "belly button." This is sought after by some variety collectors.

It should be noted that the 1878 coins and some 1879-S and 1880-CC coins show a flat eagle's breast but with feather detail instead of the round breast detail (except 1878-P reverse of 1879). Also, the 1921 Morgans have this earlier flat breast design but with less articulated feathers. Weakly struck 1921 Morgans typically show weakness in the lower wreath and roughness in the cheek area (a common problem with 1921-S).

The Peace dollar dies were not basined. From 1916 onwards the Philadelphia Mint produced all the working dies from hubs and master dies directly from the sculptured models without retouching with a graver or adding the inscriptions.[1] This preserved the detail of the original sculptor's work better and eliminated the die basining step. Thus, the weak strikes of Peace dollars are due to the original design defects or to inadequate striking pressure. The accompanying photographs show the typically weak struck hair over the ear and weak wing feathers over the legs for the 1921 Peace dollar. This was due to the difficulty in striking the coins with the initial high relief design. The first reverse design, B[1], of the 1922 with lower relief was also difficult to strike with full central detail as shown for the 1922-S.

A related weak strike problem is **planchet striations**. These show as parallel lines on the cheek of 1878-S with whiteness of the original planchet surface visible between these lines. They also appear on some Carson City issues. Planchet striations are due to weak strikes that do not fully force the planchet against all of the die cavity. The lines on the planchet were caused by rough edges of the jaws of the draw benches used to obtain the final planchet strip thickness in pre-1921 Morgan dollar production (except after 1901 at Philadelphia Mint when they were no longer used).

During the striking of coins, extraneous material sometimes came between the planchet and dies. This caused indentations in the resulting coin. The extraneous material was usually slivers or chips of silver, grease with dirt present in the presses or wood chips from the planchet drying operations.

Excessive polishing of the Morgan dies during the basining process sometimes removed part of the design. The missing design would be near the coin's field rather than the design high points for a weak strike. On

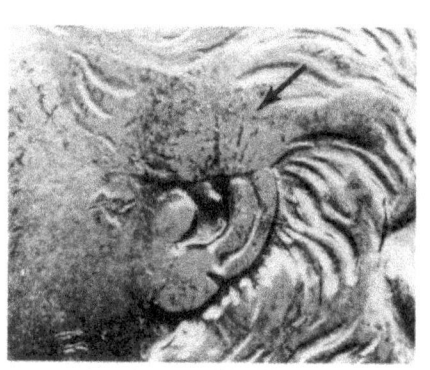

Morgan Flat Ear

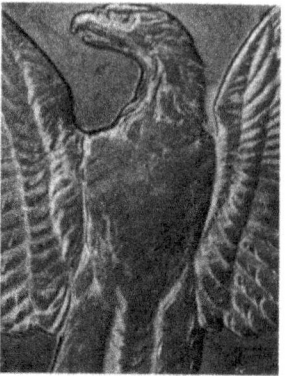

Flat Eagle's Breast

Weak Struck Reverse
with Belly Button

Belly Button Reverse

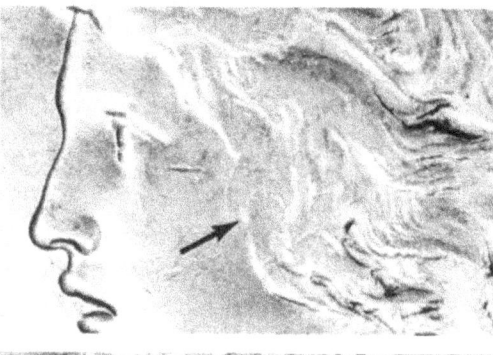

1921-P Peace
Weak Hair and
Eagle's Wing
Feathers

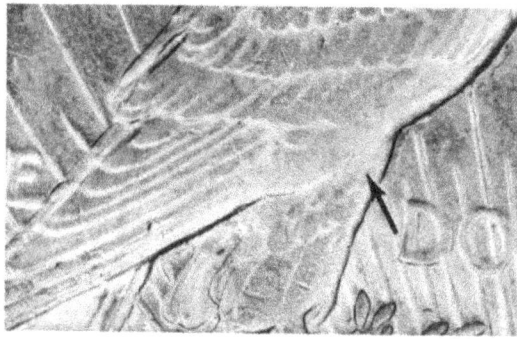

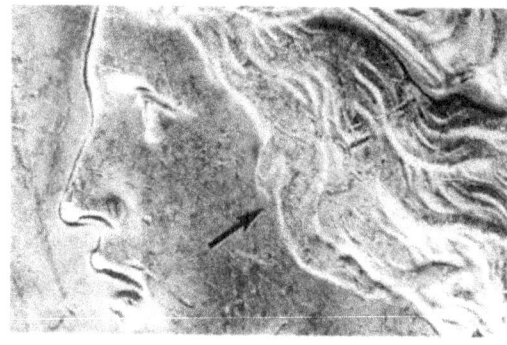

1922-S
Weak Hair and
Eagle's Wing
Feathers

Planchet Striations

Planchet Striations

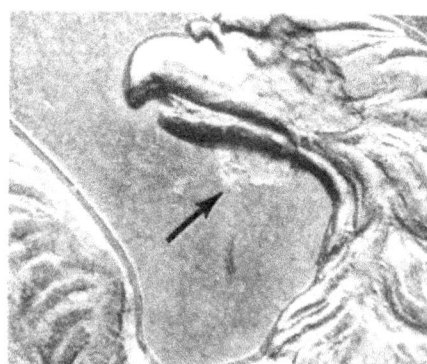

Strike Through

the obverse this shows as shallow stars and lettering or missing portions of the lower hair. On the reverse, some of the leaves became disconnected in the wreath or feathers were missing in the wing center.

LUSTER

Luster is the appearance of the original surfaces of an uncirculated coin. It varies by date, mint and even at a given mint for a particular year. For that matter it even varies within an original bag of 1,000 dollars since

Typical S-Mint Rounded Rim

Typical O-Mint Square Rim

in making up a bag, it was common practice to mix heavy and light weight tolerance coins from different press strikings to obtain the total bag weight tolerance of two hundredths of an ounce.

New Morgan dies had polished fields due to basining and a texture on the surfaces on the devices from the reducing lathe and subsequent touch-up by the engraver. It is this polished field that gives a clear definition between the devices and field. Since silver is the most reflective of all metals, the fields of the Morgan dollar have a mirror appearance on early strikes of new dies. There was some variance from year to year and mint to mint on the degree of reflectivity of the field due to how carefully the workman basined the dies and how fine a polishing compound was used in the last basining step.

As the dies wore from striking the coins, the polished field surface became dull. The mirror surface soon disappeared, replaced by brilliant non-reflective surfaces. Through continued wear the edges of the field became rough with parallel radial microscopic grooves in the die from constant planchet metal flow against the die surfaces out towards the rim.

Near the end of the die life, die chips appeared around the stars and outer lettering and die cracks often showed up through this outer lettering. Thus the fields of Morgan coins have a varied appearance depending upon at what point they were struck during a die's lifetime. A small percentage show mirror or proof-like fields. Low mintage dates tended to have predominantly brilliant field coins while high mintage dates tended to have mostly rough fields because of the lengthy use of the dies to achieve the high mintages.

There were exceptions to this however. For example, the Philadelphia Mint struck around 20 million Morgan dollars each year from 1885 through 1890. But about 50% more dies were used in the earlier years of 1885 to 1887 than 1888 to 1890. So the coins of 1888 to 1890 tend to have a greater proportion with rough dull fields. On the other hand, the early San Francisco coins of 1878 through 1882 had mintages of half the 1888 to 1890-P using almost twice as many dies! So these early S mint coins have mostly brilliant fields with a larger proportion of proof-likes. As an average number of coins struck per die pair for the entire Morgan series, the Philadelphia Mint had the highest average with over 210,000; the New Orleans Mint the next highest with about 150,000; San Francisco Mint had 121,000; and the Carson City Mint had the lowest with 64,000. From this it is obvious why the CC and S Morgan dollars tend to have more brilliant fields than the P mint dollars.

The luster on the Liberty Head and eagle varied from deep frosted to brilliant. This depended not only upon the state of the working die, but also upon the amount of wear on the working hubs and master die. Through wear the devices of a working die would normally change from a frosted look to one with dull spots. Eventually most of the frosting would give way to a brilliant look over most of the device surface from the die wearing smooth. Some heavily worn dies would even show rough areas at the edges of the devices such as neck and chin of the Liberty Head and wing tips of the eagle.

Throughout the years the master die and working hubs also accumulated wear on the devices which reduced their frostiness. Since the working hubs had to be replaced every year or two, the working dies made from them showed considerable variance in the frostiness of the devices. For example, the 1879-S and 1880-S coins are fairly common with deep cameo devices whereas the 1881-S cameo is fairly scarce. Apparently most of the 1881-S working dies were made from a worn hub with brilliant devices whereas the 1879-S and 1880-S came from new hubs. There are a few 1881-S with deep cameo devices that must have been from another new working hub.

Over the years the master die lost most of its frostiness of the devices. By the late 1890's, the device frostiness was considerably less than that of the early S mint coins. And by the turn of the century only a little frosting remained. By 1903 and 1904, virtually all of the device frosting was gone so that the proof-like and even the proof coins had little contrast between the devices and fields with mostly brilliant surfaces on the devices.

Original coin luster is best seen by tilting the coin under a light. A radial bright bar will sweep around the coin as it is tilted. This is the so called "cartwheel" effect and is caused by light being reflected off the original surface texture. A worn polished coin with smooth surfaces will not show as pronounced a cartwheel effect since the surface texture will have been changed. This is an easy and almost automatic test used by experienced collectors and dealers to tell if there is any wear on the

Cameo   Frosted   Some Frosting

Brilliant   Some Frosting   Brilliant

Deep Frosting with
Dark Patches

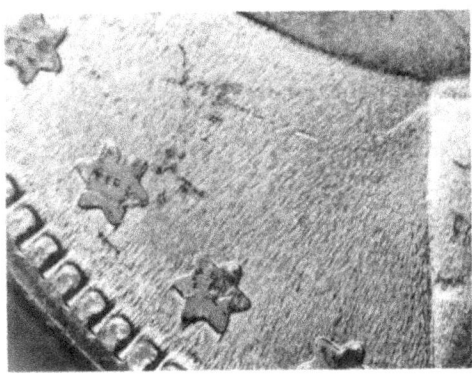

Worn Die

coin's surface. Any wear on the high points or in the fields will show up as dull areas with little luster or cartwheel effect.

To most people the heavy frosted devices combined with brilliant proof-like fields have the most desirable appearance. This produces a cameo effect with the design standing out in contrast to the fields. The frostiness of the devices and brilliance of the fields varies with the year and mint and even within a given year and mint. There is a continuous spectrum of frostiness from cameo to deep frosted to some frosting to brilliant of the devices for most years and mints. The fields varied from brilliant to dull to rough looking. Early Morgan dollars tend to show the whole range of luster spectrum of the devices and fields. Later year Morgan dollars and high mintage years have fewer examples of frosted devices and brilliant fields. Occasionally there are examples of such deep frosted devices that light and dark patches can be seen to appear across the Liberty head as the coin is tilted (evident on some 79-S and 80-S). But on the other hand, the deep frosted devices tend to show the bag marks and frost breaks more prominent than brilliant devices.

Peace dollars in general have much less frosting on the devices and less brilliance in the fields than the Morgan dollar. The entire design including peripheral lettering was reduced from the Galvano to the master die. The master die was not retooled or touched up to preserve the exact quality and texture of the original sculptor's work.[2] Thus, the surfaces of the Peace design devices and lettering tended to be smoothed out and rounded off because of the reducing lathe design transfer step. The Morgan design, on the other hand, was extensively touched up on the master die and hub causing a rougher texture which resulted in more frostiness. The lettering, stars, date and wreath were punched separately into the master die resulting in rough surfaces for tops of these parts of the design and much sharper corners and detail.

The Peace dollar die fields were not basined so their fields were rougher in texture than the Morgan

fields which were basined for each working die. Also, the Peace dollar dies struck more coins per die than the average Morgan dollar die so the Peace dollar coins in most cases show more roughness in the field and on the devices due to die wear. There are however, some Peace dollar coins that show quite a bit of frosting in the hair and on the eagle with fairly brilliant fields from early strikes of the dies.

In recent years, artificial cameo Morgan dollars have surfaced on the market. These have deep frosted Liberty Heads and in some cases the eagle. To most experienced collectors and dealers they are unnatural looking and can generally be easily spotted. There are several known methods to produce an artificial frosting on the coin surface. The crudest looking is one that has had a silvery white paint applied to the surface. It produces a thick looking and even appearance. There are usually areas of paint applied to the field or missing on the devices causing the frosting to not exactly follow the devices outline. Of course, the bag marks, scrapes, and frost breaks are also covered in this artificial frosting process producing a "cleaner" looking coin. But since these abrasions occurred after the coin was struck, they should always have shiny contact surfaces on untampered coins. Original frosting always has some degree of change across the Liberty Head surfaces becoming less pronounced closer to the coin's rim. In most cases the painted on frost will easily rub off or dissolve readily with denatured alcohol.

Another method to create artificial frosting is to silver plate the surfaces. This leaves excess silver in the

Die Polishing Lines in Field

crevices of the design, and of course, also creates frosted bag marks. A third method is to lightly sandblast the surface with a very fine abrasive to create the surface roughness. It produces an even texture with again frosted bag marks. If in doubt about a deep frosted coin, always examine the surface with a magnifying glass to see if the scratches, bag marks, scrapes and scuff marks have frosting within them.

In some cases the coins show fine raised dots of metal all over the Liberty Head and/or eagle. This is particularly common for 1883-P and 1883-O. It is due to rusted dies. The rust can occur during the storage of the die if the steel face is not protected (generally petroleum jelly is applied to die faces). Rust causes pits in the die resulting in raised spots on the coin. It gives a slightly rough texture and appearance to the coin. In some instances the rust spots may appear only on a small localized area. Coins struck from rusted dies are in most cases unchanged in value compared to those struck from normal dies as the overall appearance is little changed.

Sometimes fine hairlines are present on the fields. These can be from die polishing lines or from polishing lines or scratches put on the coin after it was minted. Die polishing lines appear as raised lines on the coins and they run up to the edges of the devices and through the middle of the lettering since the field was the high point of the dies. Polishing lines on the coin however, usually do not go up to the edges of the devices and lettering since these areas were protected from any cloth or other wiping material by the raised design. Polishing lines are best detected by tilting the coin under a light to show their presence at the proper reflecting angle. Die polishing lines usually do not affect the coin's grade or value but coin hairlines do, as previously discussed under abrasions. However, obvious die polishing lines in proof-like fields may cause it to only grade semi-PL instead of full PL.

COLOR

Color of a silver dollar refers to anything other than the natural silver brilliance. A coating on the coin surface can take the form of natural or artificial toning, dirt, grease, carbon spots, impure metal streaks, so-called water spots, cloudiness and even finger prints. Most people prefer the natural brilliance of silver. Attractive toning can enhance the beauty of a silver dollar to some people and thus its value. But the other surface coatings and imperfections can decrease the value of a coin if it is noticeable and distracting to the eye.

Toning is a color on the surface of the coin that can be localized in one area or cover an entire side or both sides. It is most often caused by chemical reactions of sulfur and silver to produce a thin film of tarnish on the coin's surface. The thin film results in various colors through a phenomenon called thin film interference. The incoming light wave is reflected off the toned surface and again below the surface on the silver coin. These two reflected waves of light then set up interference light waves to create the various colors depending on the thickness of the thin film coating.

Sulfur that tones silver dollars was present in the canvas bags that the mints and banks used to store them in. Over a period of many years, the coins against the canvas would become toned. Usually this toning would be one-sided or in crescent shapes if the coins overlapped others. The toning would be varied depending upon the thickness of the tarnish film and can be one solid color such as light golden or russet. Most often there would be several colors on one coin such as golden, rose, green, and blue. Occasionally, beautiful rainbow bands or crescents can also be found.

Sulfur was also present in the paper used to wrap rolls and in individual coin envelopes. The latter often caused toning on both sides of the coin. A roll of 20 coins wrapped in paper could cause the end coins to be toned on one side in a segmented fashion due to the overlapped folded paper. The middle coins in a roll sometimes ended up with light peripheral toning.

Toning can enhance the value of a coin if it is an attractive rainbow, vivid bands or light delicate shades. Grey or very dark toning is generally considered undesirable and can decrease the value of a coin. The desirability of toned coins is very much a personal preference and not all collectors and dealers like them.

Buyers of toned coins have to be particularly careful that the toning is not hiding excessive abrasions, weak strikes, hairlines or other defects. A toned coin should be carefully examined to determine its true grade in terms of abrasions, strike, luster and any proof-like tendencies. A magnifying glass can be helpful in trying to look through the toning to the coin's surface. Tilting the coin under a good light is also very helpful for the examination.

Toning can also be artificially applied to coins by various means. Artificial toning means any treatment of the coin's surface that creates toning in a few seconds to a few days. So-called natural toning generally takes many months or many years to create the delicate colors from coin contact with the canvas bags, roll wrappers and paper envelopes. The tarnishing of silver can be speeded up by subjecting the coin to hot humid weather, storage in a polluted city or near factory atmospheres, exposure to sunlight, or exposure to atmospheres with high sulphur or sulfate content. Such abuse of coins may be accidental or intentional – one would generally never

Toned Dollar

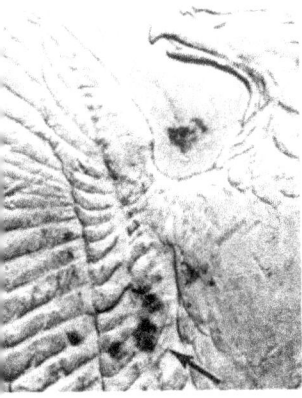

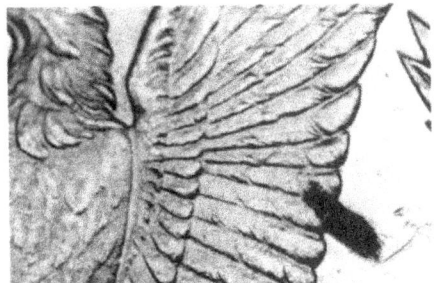

Impure Metal Streak

Carbon Spots

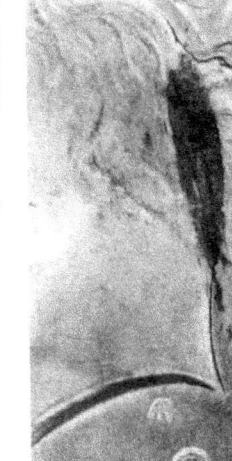

Impure Metal Streak

know which was the case.

There are chemical baths that the coin can be immersed in to cause tarnish coatings within seconds or minutes. Of course such treatment causes both sides of the coin to be toned. Or, the solution can be brushed on to only one side. Generally, the resultant toning has a thick splotchy look that is usually easy to tell from the more delicate and even natural toning. There have even been cases of paints applied to the surfaces but their thick texture causes a very unnatural look. Also, the tars in cigarette smoke can impart a light coating. On a naturally toned coin, however, the coin's luster always shines through the toning.

Because of the long term storage of many of the Morgan and Peace dollars and their transportation all over the country by various means, they are frequently coated with **dirt, dust and grease**. The canvas storage bags were not airtight. In addition, many millions of the coins were re-bagged from time to time as their original bags rotted or split. Such dirt and grease coatings can be easily seen by simply placing the coin upright under a light on a plain piece of white paper. By looking at the coin any coating on its surface will be apparent as areas darker than the normal silver luster. A light dirt or grease coating does not affect the coin's value, but a heavy coating that is distracting in appearance can lower the coin's value.

Small roundish dark areas on a coin's surface are commonly called **carbon spots**. These are localized corrosion and tarnished areas. Usually they are due to an impurity speck imbedded in the coin's surface which causes an active corrosive spot surrounded by toned rings. This impurity speck can be from impurities present in the silver melt which end up near or on the coin's surface. Or, foreign particles such as dust, tobacco, paper specks and airborne contaminants can become lodged against a coin's surface and cause a corrosive action to take place. Some carbon spots are very active and continue to grow with time. Others are stable and do not change size. Sometimes careful removal of the surface contaminant followed by local application of tarnish removal solution will completely remove a carbon spot.

If the impurity is imbedded into the surface, then it is likely that the tarnish spot will reappear within weeks or months after its removal. Also, removal of the imbedded impurity will leave a small cavity in the surface.

Small carbon spots that require a magnifying glass to detect do not affect the value of a coin. But if there are many of these microscopic spots or the carbon spots are readily visible to the naked eye, then the coin's value is decreased. Most collectors, dealers and investors shun coins with obvious large carbon spots which reduces their value considerably.

Related to carbon spots are the **impure metal streaks**. These are due to slag trapped in the silver ingots. Slag is melt impurities that float to the top of the melt with the flux and charcoal (used to coat the top of the melt and reduce exposure to the atmospheric oxygen). The flux with impurities was supposed to have been skimmed off each melt before its pouring. Also, in pouring the melt into the ingot mold, any flux and charcoal should have floated to the top within the end gate which was later trimmed off. But, occasionally, some flux and charcoal material get trapped within the ingot. When this ingot was later rolled into strips, the impurity became flattened and elongated into a streak. If this streak was on the planchet surface the struck coin would show an elongated dark area.

Since the impure metal streak is made up of impurities imbedded in the coin metal there is no known method to remove these impurities without leaving a rough depressed area. Commercial dips will not affect an impure metal streak except perhaps remove any peripheral toning. Large unsightly impure metal streaks can make a coin very difficult to sell, thus greatly lowering its value. In general, coins with distracting impure metal streaks should be avoided or only purchased at reduced prices.

Water Spots are light whitish areas that appear on some of the early Peace dollars. These whitish areas are not simply surface coatings, but are etched into the coin's surface. Thus, the commercial coin dips have no effect on them. A possible cause of these spots could be inadequate rinsing and drying of the planchets after their being whitened in a mild sulfuric acid bath following the planchet annealing operation. Again, the presence of

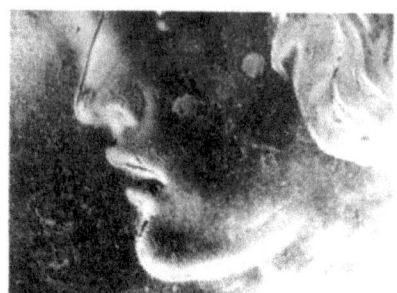
Water Spots

large distracting water spot areas can lower a coin's value whereas a couple of small insignificant spots may not.

Occasionally, a coin may have a slight **cloudiness** on one or both sides of a coin which dulls the luster. Upon close examination with a magnifying glass light white to yellow streaks and spots can be seen. Generally, this cloudiness is embedded in the coin's surface and commercial coin dips will not move it. The exact cause of the cloudiness is not known but could be due to the inadequate rinsing of the planchets, PVC from soft plastic holders or the results of severe tarnishing of the coins. The reduction in the coin's value depends on how severe the original surface luster has been subdued.

Through the mishandling of coins, **fingerprints** get imparted on them. Perspiration from the fingers contain acids which, if left on the coin, can cause the fingerprint pattern to be permanently etched into the coin's surface. This leaves a series of white parallel lines on the coin which cannot be removed by any commercial dip. Fresh fingerprints of a few months or less can sometimes be successfully removed by these dips, however. The location and extent of the fingerprints will determine how distracting they are and thus the effect on the coin's value. Of course, to avoid fingerprints on coins, they should only be handled by their edges.

PROOF-LIKE COINS

The term proof-like refers to the degree of reflection that can be seen in the field of a business strike coin. Since the nineteenth century proof coins and the early and late twentieth century proof coins had highly reflective fields, the similarity in appearance of business strike coins with reflective fields gave rise to the term proof-like.

Although the degree of reflection in a coin's field required for the term proof-like to apply has not been standardized, it is common practice to require a clear reflection of at least two to four inches. That is a distance at which an object in front of the coin can be clearly discerned in the coin's field.

Many methods are used for the reflectance test including a finger tip, eyeball, and printed matter. These methods do not provide a very standardized test so the authors have devised a Morgan Dollar Proof-Like Guide. This Guide has pairs of resolution lines running the

length of a card for the distance of eight inches with various terms along the length of the lines. These terms are between pairs of lines running cross-wise on the Guide to define the Semi Proof-Like (SPL), Proof-Like (PL), and Deep Mirror Proof-Like (DMPL) distances. SPL has been defined as a reflection of one to two inches. Any reflection less than one inch is deemed not sufficient to be defined as SPL. PL is a reflection of two to four inches. DMPL is a reflection of four inches to the card's end of eight inches. Clear reflection beyond eight inches is sometimes referred to as Very Deep Mirror PL, Super DMPL, Ultra DMPL, incredible DMPL, mile mirrors, or some other superlatives. Since silver is the most reflective of all metals, the surfaces of the silver dollar fields can in rare instances have virtually a perfect mirror that one can see their face at practically any distance!

To be graded and valued as a proof-like, the Morgan silver dollar has to be proof-like on both sides. There are many examples of one-sided proof-likes. They are valued as non proof-likes or only slightly higher if the obverse is proof-like. Often the bright luster of the early S mint dollars will appear to be proof-like, but in actuality, will have little or no reflection in the fields. Before purchasing proof-like dollars at their premium prices, the degree of reflection should be tested for both sides of the coin.

As discussed under the luster section, the degree of frosting for proof-like dollars can range from deep cameo, to frosted, to some frosting, to brilliant. The degree of frosting and depth of the mirror come in all combinations but not for all years. This is because the frostiness of the devices depended upon the state of frostiness of the master die and working hubs as well as the working dies. The degree of proof-like of the fields depended upon the degree of mirror initially imparted during the basining of each Morgan working die as well as the degree of wear of each working die. Thus, as pointed out in the section on luster, the master die had lost much of its frostiness by the turn of the century and Morgan dollars after 1900 exhibit primarily only light frosting. But these last few years of the Morgan dollar can have very deep mirrored fields.

The early years of the Morgan dollars tended to have a higher percentage of deep mirrored cameos; especially for some of the low mintage years of the CC and S mints. But even these early years show weak PL's with light frosting and deep mirrors with light frosting. Those years with low numbers of coins struck per dies had a higher proportion of PL coins. Thus, the early S and CC coins have quite a few PL coins available. Some higher mintage years like 84-P, 89-P, and 90-P are relatively scarce in proof-like. Other years like 84-S, 93-O, 94-P, and 01-P are very scarce or virtually unknown in mint state PL which may be due to a high percentage of these coins being melted or released into circulation.

The **value** of a proof-like dollar depends upon its eye appeal. Generally, the deeper the frosting with the

S. PL Rev.   PL Rev.   D.M.PL Rev.

proof-like fields, the more contrast will be present and the higher the value. Of course the number and placement of the bag marks as well as the sharpness of the strike will affect the value of proof-like dollars. Deep mirrored cameos with full strikes and minimal marks are the most valued of Morgan dollars. But each proof-like Morgan has to be evaluated on its own merits of bag marks, strike, luster, color and depth of proof-like.

The **cause** of proof-like Morgan dollars was due to the polishing of the working dies during the initial basining process or later to polish out die clash marks. The condition of the planchet surfaces had virtually no effect on the degree of reflection in the coin's surface since during striking of the coin the planchet metal deformed and flowed into the die cavities, recesses and indentations. Business dies did not have the almost flawless mirrored fields of the proof Morgan dies. Striking of Morgan proof coins required polished and selected planchets to minimize any slight surface imperfections that might result from nicks and scratches on the planchets. But for the imperfect business die fields, the condition of the planchet surface from individual planchet polishing, smoothness of the strip rollers, or condition of the drawing bench jaws would have no effect on the degree of mirrors on the coin's field. Rough planchet surfaces could, on occasion, cause some imperfections in the form of pits or lines in the coin fields, however. Also, the constant friction of the planchet metal flow against the die surfaces gradually wore the die surfaces. But since the metal flow is generally in an outward radial direction, the die wear took the form of radial flow lines. Planchet friction against the die fields did not produce even polished die surfaces.

The sculptured models of the U.S. designs for silver coins from 1916 onwards were prepared with no intention of basining the working dies.[3] Master dies for silver coins struck prior to 1916 were lower in relief and had much greater sharpness in detail by re-engraving. In addition, they were prepared with a basined field that was polished to a perfect radius on a revolving disc.

Since the 1921 Morgan dollar was similar to the design used until 1904, it was also struck from basined working dies. Thus, there are proof-like 1921-P Morgan dollars. However, there are relatively few proof-like 1921-D and 1921-S Morgans even though they have large mintages. At some point in 1921 the mints at Philadelphia, Denver and San Francisco apparently discarded the basining step for the working dies. For the Morgan design this resulted in less than optimum striking of the coin as evidenced by many 1921-D and 1921-S with weakly struck wreath and other details. All three mints operated at full capacity in 1921 to replace as quickly as possible the silver dollars melted in 1918 and 1919 under the Pittman Act. So production shortcuts were apparently taken to achieve the highest possible production.

Basining of the Morgan dollar working dies was performed at each mint just prior to their being placed into the presses. It consisted of putting the dies upright in a fixture which held the die face against a slightly dished disc. As this disc revolved with polishing compound, it polished the die face making it slightly concave. The radius of this curvature varied with each mint and caused the planchet metal to flow more towards the coin rim or coin center in the extreme cases. The depth of the mirror on the die field was a function of how fine a compound was used during the basining process and also if a final buffing of the die face was performed. Thus, the degree of mirror initially on the working die field varied from mint to mint over the years and at a particular mint with time because of the different workmen and practices enforced.

As the basined and polished working die struck coins, the friction of the planchet metal moving against the die field would wear the die surfaces making them dull. The mirror field surfaces would gradually become less and less reflective until it became semi proof-like and finally dull with no reflection. Proof dies that are not chrome plated can strike around 2,000 coins before they are discarded with too many dull areas on the field for proof coins. So it is estimated that a proof-like Morgan working die could have struck around 5,000 to 10,000 fully proof-like coins before it became semi-proof-like or nonreflective. This represents 2 to 15% of the average production of a Morgan working die.

Morgan working dies were also occasionally polished during their lifetime to remove severe die clash marks. If the obverse and reverse dies accidently came together without a planchet between them, a portion of the design from both dies would transfer to one another. Polishing the dies to remove these clash marks resulted in mirror fields again on the dies. If the dies clashed early in the die's lifetime, some frosting may still have been present on the devices. Polishing the dies late in their lifetimes would result in proof-likes with brilliant devices.

In rare instances the Peace dollar dies were also polished to remove clash marks. This resulted in the few known weak proof-like Peace dollars with semi-proof-like and weak proof-like fields of two to three inches for the 1922-D, 1925-P, 1927-S, 1935-D, 1935-S. In practically all cases of proof-like Peace dollars the coins show evidence of die polishing lines and usually only part of the fields have any degree of reflection. As mentioned above, the Peace dollar design was not intended to utilize basined dies. But the Peace dollars frequently have die clash marks just as the Morgan dollars commonly show them. However, the Peace dollar clash marks are not as evident or severe perhaps due to the more rounded design next to the fields.

There have surfaced in recent times some dollars with artificial polished fields. These coins at first glance appear to be proof-like. But, upon closer examination, the fields do not have the same depth of mirror within the letters or near the edge of the devices. This is due to the difficulty of polishing the coin's field near the raised design. To most experienced collectors and dealers, these artificial proof-like coins are easily detected.

PROOF VERSUS PROOF-LIKE COINS

Another grading area that the buyer should beware of is a proof-like Morgan dollar being passed off as a genuine proof coin. Only 500 to 1,000 genuine Morgan proof coins were struck each year by the Philadelphia Mint (except for 1921 when about 25 were struck). A few proofs were also struck by the branch mints to commemorate special events, namely, 12 1879-O, 12 1883-O, 12 1893-CC and 24 1921-S.

All proof coins were struck under special conditions to produce an exceptional coin. New dies with fields polished to mirror finish were used. The coin planchets were also polished on both sides. These planchets were then struck twice under higher than normal pressures to produce proof coins with perfect mirror fields and exceptionally sharp detail. These proof coins were always handled separately by hand after being struck to prevent accumulating nicks and scratches.

Proof-like coins may have part or all of one side and/or both sides with a mirror-like field. Working dies for the normal Morgan dollar production had polished fields that produced coins with mirror-like fields. These dies were not as carefully polished as dies for striking proof coins. Also, the planchets did not receive special polishing. The struck coins were not individually handled by hand after injection from the dies, but instead, they fell into the hopper with other coins and were later put into canvas bags of one thousand coins. This resulted in nicks, scratches and bag marks appearing on virtually all coins. In addition, the planchet was struck only once under normal striking pressure so that the detail is not as sharp as a proof coin.

The accompanying photographs show details of the lower reverses of a proof and an exceptionally nice proof-like Morgan dollar. Note the difference in the field appearances – the proof coin has a nearly perfect mirror field with only a few die polishing marks. The proof-like field has many small blemishes, scratches and nicks. Also, the letters of the proof coin has square edges and flat tops whereas the proof-like coin has rounded edges and small dents on top. The most obvious difference is the square proof rim with no scratches, dents or abrasions and the proof-like rim rounded on the outside with many small dents. Chapter Seven notes that most Morgan proofs have unique edge reeding counts.

Proof-like fields on a coin do not change the grade of a coin. Their presence makes the coin more desirable to many collectors and thus tend to command premium prices.

GRADING PROOF SILVER DOLLARS

Grading criteria for proof Morgan and Peace silver dollars is different than that for business strike silver dollars. The proof silver dollars were individually handled by hand in removing them from the striking presses (either screw or hydraulic) and placed into envelopes. Thus, they did not accumulate bag marks like the business strikes, unless they were mishandled. Instead, the types of abrasions seen on proof dollars are tiny hairlines on the devices and/or fields, and rubbing on the high points of the devices. These are due to rubbing of the delicate surfaces by the envelope paper or rubbing with cloth by well meaning owners to remove tarnish and toning.

The strike and luster criteria apply to proof dollars as well as the business strikes. Most proof dollars were well struck and are deeply frosted or cameo. This is because they were struck twice on either a screw or hydraulic press at higher pressures than the business strikes. Also, generally less than 1,000 proof pieces were struck so the dies were new with frosting on the devices. The exceptions are the 1902 - 1904 proofs which have brilliant rather than cameo devices. Possibly, this was due to the change from wood to gas annealing furnaces for the planchets in 1901 or the master die had lost most of its frosting by that date.

A good percentage of proof dollars are toned because of their initial storage in paper envelopes. The almost perfect mirror fields were very susceptible to picking up thin tarnish films which show up as delicate toning shades. In general, toning on proof dollars does not affect the value because toning on them is so common. Exceptionally delicate and eye appealing toning can enhance the value and likewise, dark unattractive toning can lessen the value. One has to be especially careful on toned proof dollars to examine the surfaces under the toning for hairlines and rubbing.

All of the Morgan proof dollars have deep, almost perfect mirrored fields. The exception is the 1921 Zerbe proofs which do not have very deep mirrored fields. The 1921 and 1922 Peace dollar proofs do not exhibit the deep mirrored fields. Instead, they are matte or satin finish proofs with exceptionally strong strikes and sharp detail for the Peace design. Morgan proofs show full frosted hair and eagle (except 1902-1904) with very sharp hairline, cotton boll tops and eagle's feathers. Letters, stars, and date are sharp with squared edges. Rim is square and raised above sharp denticles.

Detail of Proof Reverse
Mirror field with only fine die polishing marks. Square flat-top letters and rim with no scratches, dents or abrasions.

Detail of BU Proof-Like Reverse
Mirror field has small blemishes, scratches and nicks. Letters and rim have small dents and rounded edges.

PROOF MS67 OR 68 – A virtually flawless coin with no hairlines, marks or rubbing and fully struck with outstanding luster or frosting. May have light attractive toning. Only a few proof silver dollars have survived in this condition.

PROOF MS66 – Almost flawless with only a maximum of a couple of hairlines visible under magnification on the devices or in the fields. May have barely discernable frost breaks on very high points of devices. Must have full strike and outstanding frosting and luster for date. May have light attractive toning.

PROOF MS65 – A few hairlines in fields and/or on devices and may have noticeable frost breaks on high points of devices. Sharply struck with attractive frosting and luster for date. May have attractive toning.

PROOF MS63 – Numerous hairlines in fields and/or on devices in large areas with obvious frost breaks on high points of devices. A few marks or scratches may be evident. Strike may be weak and frosting and luster may be noticeably subdued for date. May have toning that is very heavy, splotchy, dark or otherwise unattractive.

Proof Obverse and Reverse

PROOF MS60 – Excessive hairlines and polishing over most of coin surfaces. Distracting marks or scratches may be present. Strike may be weak and frosting and luster may be dull for date. May have unattractive toning.

PROOF CIRCULATED – A few proof silver dollars managed to get into circulation. In describing their grades the term proof is added before the circulated grade designation and the wear characteristics for business strike circulated grades are utilized.

GRADING MORGAN SILVER DOLLARS

Each of the grading criteria of abrasions, strike, luster, color and proof-like must be considered when grading uncirculated Morgan silver dollars. Wear is the primary grading criteria when grading circulated dollars.

For the Morgan dollar the cheek area of the Liberty Head is the most critical area for examining for abrasions since it is a flat open area in the center of the obverse. The eagle on the reverse is less likely to show abrasions because of the feather detail. Coins with distracting large abrasions on the cheek will never grade above MS63. Likewise, coins with obvious missing hair detail above the Liberty Head ear and very weak detail on the eagle's breast feathers will not grade above MS63. Any toning or proof-like tendencies should be added to the grade description.

A grading number can be assigned to both sides of the coin. However, a single number or adjective designation is more widely used and most price guides use a single number/designation. If the two sides grade differently, then the lower grade is assigned as the overall coin grade. However, usually emphasis is on the obverse grade.

MS70 – A flawless coin just as it came out of the press with full strike and outstanding luster. No known Morgan business strike coins meet this criteria.

MS66 – No bag marks or other abrasions on Liberty Head cheek visible to naked eye and only a few small abrasions elsewhere. Fully struck with exceptional luster and brilliant fields to give an overall exceptional appearance. Emphasis is on obverse.

MS65 – Only a few small, non-distracting bag marks or other abrasions on cheek visible to the naked eye with no large scratches, digs or scuff marks elsewhere. Sharply struck on both sides with good luster and bright to brilliant fields to give over all pleasing appearance. Emphasis is on obverse.

MS64 – May have a couple of small, somewhat distracting bag marks on the cheek visible to the naked eye. May show slight weakness in the strike. Luster is average or better with good overall appearance. Emphasis still on obverse.

MS63 – Some obvious bag marks, scratches, or scuff marks on cheek and in fields and design areas. May be weakly struck and darkly toned or have dull luster or dull fields due to worn dies. Appearance is still fairly good with emphasis on obverse.

MS66   MS65

MS63   MS60

MS60 – Significant and numerous bag marks, scratches, or scuff marks on cheek and elsewhere. Other characteristics such as weak strike, dull luster, unsightly toning, or other problems may detract from coin's appearance.

50 ABOUT UNCIRCULATED (AU)

Note: Slight but continuous wear in front areas of Liberty Head cheek and neck, center of obverse and reverse fields. Most of mint luster is present.

AU Obverse

I & II Obv.	Traces of wear on hair above ear, edges of cotton leaves, tops of cotton bolls, top of cap.
III Obv.	Traces of wear on hair above ear, edges of cotton leaves and top of cap; half of detail on cotton boll tops gone.
IV Obv.	Traces of wear on hair above and below ear and on top of cap; one third of detail on cotton boll tops gone.

AU Reverse

A, B, D Rev.	Trace of wear on eagle's breast, wing tips and on lines on top of eagle's legs; detail on eagle's talons smooth.
C Rev.	Center feathers on eagle's breast worn smooth; trace of wear on wing tips and on lines on top of eagle's legs; details on talons smooth.

EF Obverse

All Obv.   Slight worn spots on hair above date, ear and below LIBERTY; little detail left on cotton boll tops; slight flat spots on very edges of cotton leaves. Light wear on cheek. Partial mint luster should be present.

VF Obverse

All Obv.   Smooth spots on all hair from forehead to ear; lower and upper cotton leaves smooth but all are separated; wear on wheat stalk grains; cross lines on cotton bolls have smooth areas.

EF Reverse

A, B, D Rev.   Only a few feathers remain across the eagle's breast; top of eagle's legs smooth; talons slightly flat; top leaves of wreath have traces of wear; feathers on eagle's head and neck slightly worn; wing tips show flat spots.

C rev.   Same as above except eagle's breast show feathers only at the side. Partial mint luster still present.

VF Reverse

All Rev.   Smooth parts on eagle's wing; breast smooth; few feathers show on neck; talons are flat; cross point of the olive branch and arrow shafts still distinct; some of leaves in wreath are worn flat.

12-15 FINE (F)

7, 8, 10 VERY GOOD (VG)

F Obverse

All Obv. Hair above forehead mostly smooth but outlined; lower two cotton leaves worn together but distinct from cap; some wheat stalk grains smooth; cotton bolls flat but two lines from stem show.

VG Obverse

All Obv. All the design and the inscriptions will be very clear. Fine detail in hair lacking; hair merges with face above ear; cotton leaves flat and two lower ones merge with cap; abrasions. cotton bolls show no detail; rim still distinct.

F Reverse

All Rev. One-quarter of eagle's right wing and edge of left wing smooth; eagle's head, neck and breast flat and joined; cross point of olive branch and arrow shafts not distinct; tail feathers show slight wear; all top leaves in wreath are flat.

VG Reverse

All Rev. One-half of eagle's right wing and one third of left wing smooth; leaves in wreath are all worn; olive branch and arrow shafts are flat; rim still distinct.

4, 5, 6 GOOD (G)

The date, all of the letters and devices will have clear outlines. All of Liberty's hair and most of the detail on the eagle worn smooth. Rim will be worn down to tops of letters and will be flat to field of coin in a few places.

3 ABOUT GOOD (AG)

Date will be clear and most all of the design outline of the coin will be clearly legible although some faint areas will be present. Coin as a whole will be worn nearly smooth with rim flat and merging into field in many places.

2 FAIR (FR)

Date and more than half of the legend and inscription will be readable. Rim will be worn flat in most places.

1 BASAL STATE – POOR

Identifiable as a silver dollar but badly worn with only a portion of the legend or inscription legible. Partial date and no mutilation.

GRADING PEACE SILVER DOLLARS

The grading criteria of abrasions, strike, luster and color are also used to grade uncirculated Peace silver dollars. Proof-like is normally not used since any Peace dollars with proof-like tendencies are extremely rare. Wear is also the primary criteria when grading circulated dollars.

For the Peace dollar, the cheek area is also the most important area for examining for abrasions. But it is a smaller area than that of the Morgan dollar whereas the neck area is much larger and about the same size as the cheek area. So, for the Peace dollar, the cheek and neck area both have to be examined first for abrasions.

On the Peace dollar reverse, the eagle's right wing comprises a large area. The feather detail is not as articulated as that on the Morgan dollar wings and thus show bag marks, scrapes, and scratches more easily. The eagle's wing on the Peace dollar is therefore an important area to examine for abrasions; more so than the Morgan dollar eagle.

The more rounded design with less detail of the Peace dollar makes it more difficult to detect any wear on the high points. The high points of the hair, cheek, and neck on the obverse and the upper part of the eagle's right wing and head on the reverse should be carefully examined for dullness or hairlines indicating wear. Tilting the coin under a strong light and using a magnifying glass for close examination is often necessary to detect light circulation wear.

Weak strikes show as flat and rough texture on the hair over the Liberty Head ear and on the eagle's upper leg feathers and the wing feathers just above the legs. Obvious weakness in these areas will preclude a Peace dollar from grading MS65. The majority of high relief 1921 Peace design coins are weakly struck.

Many Peace dollars show dull luster due to a granular surface texture. This is caused by excessive die wear from extended use of the dies. Peace dollars with brilliant fields and some frosting in the hair and on the eagle from early strikes of the dies are more attractive and thus more desirable and valuable.

MS70 – A flawless coin just as it came out of the press with full strike and outstanding luster. No known Peace business strike coins meet this condition.

MS66 – No bag marks or other abrasions on Liberty Head cheek and neck visible to naked eye and only a few small abrasions elsewhere. Fully struck with exceptional luster and brilliant fields to give an overall exceptional appearance. Emphasis is on obverse.

MS65 – Only a few small bag marks or other abrasions on cheek, neck and eagle's wing visible to naked eye with no large scratches, digs or scuff marks elsewhere. Sharply struck on both sides with good luster and bright to brilliant fields to give overall pleasing appearance. Emphasis is on obverse.

MS64 – May have a couple of small, somewhat distracting bag marks on the cheek visible to the naked eye. May show slight weakness in the strike. Luster is average or better with good overall appearance. Emphasis still on obverse.

MS63 – Some obvious bag marks, scratches, or scuff marks on cheek, neck, eagle's wing and in fields and design areas. May be weakly struck and darkly toned or have dull luster or dull fields due to worn dies. Appearance is still fairly good with emphasis on obverse.

MS60 – Significant and numerous bag marks, scratches, or scuff marks an cheek, and elsewhere. Other characteristics such as weak strike, dull luster, unsightly toning, or other problems may detract from coin's appearance.

MS66   MS65

AU Obverse

I Obv.   Hair detail lacking over ear, even on uncirculated specimens; slight wear evident on hair above forehead.

II Obv.   Trace of wear on hair over ear and above forehead.

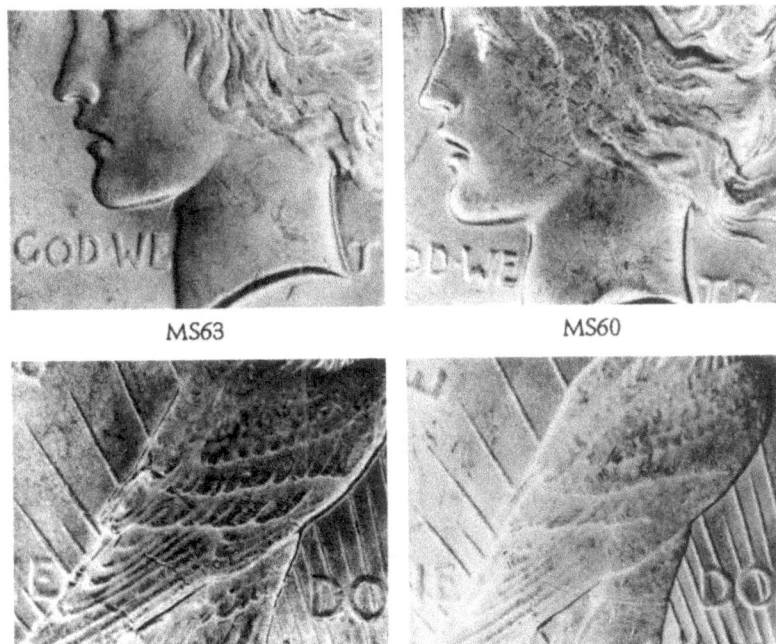

MS63   MS60

AU Reverse

All Rev.   Trace of wear on top and outside edge of eagle's right wing.

Note: Slight but continuous wear in front areas of Liberty Head cheek and neck, center of obverse and reverse fields. Most of mint luster is present.

EF Obverse

All Obv.   Wear on all hair around the face, but many fine hair strands still show around the ear and head band. Light wear on cheek and neck. Partial mint luster still present.

VF Obverse

All Obv.   Very little hair detail left around the face; front curl slightly worn.

EF Reverse

All Rev.   Slight wear on eagle's right wing and legs; trace of wear on eagle's head behind the eye and on top of the neck. Partial mint luster present.

VF Reverse

All Rev.   Much feather detail missing on right wing, but the three horizontal lines of feather layers still show, wear on neck and leg feathers; trace of wear on E PLURIBUS lettering.

12-15 FINE (F)

F Obverse

All Obv.   All hair around the face is smooth; slight wear on hair at the back of head and on the cap, trace of wear on the rays.

F Reverse

All Rev.   All of lower horizontal line of feather layers still show, but others weak or missing; no feather detail on right leg and only lower third of neck feathers show; portion of PEACE and E PLURIBUS weak.

7, 8, 10 VERY GOOD (VG)

VG Obverse

All Rev.   Hair is flattened and rays have flat spots, portions of IN GOD weak.

VG Reverse

All Rev.   No horizontal line of feather layers remain; flat spots on right leg, wing and upper neck and head; few feathers on lower neck show; portions of rays, PEACE and E PLURIBUS missing.

4, 5-6 GOOD (G)

The date, Liberty Head, and eagle outline will be clear. Portions of IN GOD, PEACE and E PLURIBUS will be missing. Rim will be worn to top of letters and will be flat to field of coin in a few places.

3 ABOUT GOOD (AG)

Date will be clear and most all of the design outline of coin will be clearly legible although faint areas will be present. Coin as a whole will be worn nearly smooth, with rim flat and merging into the field in many places.

2 FAIR (FR)

Date will be weak and at least half of the legend and inscription will be readable. Rim will be worn flat to the field in most places.

1 BASAL STATE – POOR

Identifiable as a silver dollar but badly worn with only a portion of legend or inscription legible. Partial date and no mutilation.

Footnotes

[1] Nellie Tayloe Ross, Director of the Mint, "The 1936 Proof Coins," *The Numismatist*, July 1936, p. 531.

[2] Ibid.

[3] Ibid.

The dollar collectors may want to photograph their coins for a variety of reasons. Particularly valuable specimens may need full coin photographs for positive identification in case of theft through the unique scratches, bag marks, and polishing lines on each coin. Enlargement photographs of the date, mint mark, or other areas may be needed to send to other collectors or authenticators to verify particular varieties. Special photographs may also be needed to publish in periodicals or books. Rather than have these photographs taken by a commercial photographer, excellent photographs can be made by most anyone using suitable amateur photographic equipment.

CAMERAS

The modern Single Lens Reflex (SLR) 35 mm camera is by far the most suitable camera available to the average collector for taking extreme close-up pictures of coins. In recent years this type camera has become readily available at moderate prices to the amateur photographer. Modern lens, films, and photographic papers allow date and mint mark pictures taken by 35 mm cameras to be enlarged to 8 x 10 inch size with little loss of detail. The modern SLR 35 mm camera boasts of such features as through the lens viewing, ground glass focusing, through the lens metering, interchangeable lens, and a wide range of lens and accessories readily available. These features make it easier to obtain good close-up pictures.

Other types of cameras such as the 35 mm range finder and 120 twin lens reflex can also take close-up pictures, but they are not as convenient as the 35 mm SLR. These other type cameras are more difficult to focus and obtain correct exposures. Taking good pictures with them takes longer, requires experimentation, and results in some wasted film frames. So this chapter will concentrate in using the SLR 35 mm camera.

There are many good makes and models of the SLR 35 mm camera on the market. The very cheapest should be avoided because of poor construction, reliability and lens quality. Likewise, an expensive one is not required. A moderately priced camera with interchangeable lens and through the lens metering would be adequate. It is the selection of the lens and other equipment for close-up photography that poses the greatest challenge.

LENS

This section surveys the various lens and equipment that can be used for close-up photography of coins. Hopefully this will enable the reader to buy items specifically suited to their purpose and thus avoid buying useless, inferior, or expensive lens and equipment through hit or miss and experimentation techniques.

Generally, coin photography falls into two categories; whole coin photos and extreme close-up photos of just a portion of a coin. Whole coin photos require a coin image size on a 35 mm film negative of up to about 1/2 times life size for a silver dollar and up to about 1-1/2 times life size for smaller coins. Extreme close-ups begin at about 2 times life size and can go to 25 times life size or more.

Lens and equipment combinations for coin photography can be categorized as follows:

- Normal and macro lens unassisted
- Supplementing normal lens
- Extending normal lens
- Reversing normal lens
- Special flat field lens
- Microscopes

An excellent pamphlet on this subject is *Close Up Photography* by William J. Owens as part of the Petersen Photo Publishing Group that is available at most photography stores. Although the treatment is general in nature, most of the discussion can be applied to coin photography.

The following sub-sections survey the performance of lens and associated equipments for close-up photography. There are two sets of photographs showing the test results of each combination of lens and equipment. One set shows the size of a silver dollar in an actual 35 mm negative size. The other set shows the enlarged photographs of the U.S. Air Force test photo charts to show any distortion. All test photographs were shot at an aperture of f/8.

Normal and Macro Lens

Most normal focal length lens for the Single Lens Reflex (SLR) 35 mm camera are about 50 to 55 mm and can focus down to about 18 inches from the subject. At this distance, a silver dollar appears about 1/5 life size on the 35 mm film negative. This is hardly large enough to obtain detailed full size coin prints and certainly not of sufficient size to obtain detailed close-ups of a date or mint mark.

A macro lens can be focused closer than a normal lens to permit about 1/2 life size of the film negative. It can take normal pictures and snap shots in addition to close-up shots. Extended focusing of the lens enables the macro lens to achieve this versatility. It can thus take excellent whole coin shots but is lacking the capability to take extreme close-ups of dates and mint marks. Macro lens are not cheap and can run $75 – $100 and upwards.

Supplementing Normal Lens

An easy and inexpensive way to enable a normal camera lens to focus closer is to use supplementary close-up lenses. These are single lens that screw in the front of the normal lens. They can be obtained in varying strengths usually expressed in diopters from +1 to +10 or +20. The diopter rating is the reciprocal of the focal length in meters.

Usually the close-up lenses come in sets of 3 in +1, +2, and +4 diopters. They can be used singly or in combinations with the highest strength put next to the normal camera lens. There are also available variable close-up lens that have a range of 1/5 to 1/2 life size on the 35 mm negative.

The accompanying diagram and photos show some typical results of photographing silver dollars with close-up lens. Using the +1, +2 and +4 close-up lens in combination, the silver dollar just fills the 35 mm negative. However, because of the multiple lens surfaces, flare became a problem (reduced contrast due to multiple light reflections off the various lens surfaces). The +10 close-up lens was 1/1.3 life-size but introduced some edge distortion. Distortion was severe at the edges for the +20 close-up lens. Flare and distortion was much less severe for the variable close-up lens.

Close-up lens are thus useful for making whole coin photos and coin close-ups showing about ½ to ¼ of a silver dollar. Flare can be a problem when using combinations of close-up lens. The stronger close-up lens

of +10 and +20 have distortion at the edges because of curvature of the field and are only useful at the center part of the negative.

Extending Normal Lens

Increased magnification can be obtained by extending the normal lens further away from the camera body. It creates a larger image at the film plane and also enables focusing down to a shorter distance. The extension device is merely a light tight tube between the camera body and the normal camera lens. They are available in two convenient forms, the extension tubes and bellows.

Since no lens elements are added, flare is not increased over that of the normal lens. At higher magnification distortion can become a problem. However, the exposure must be increased as the extension becomes greater because the effective "f-number" of the lens is made greater. An "f-number" is the ratio of the lens diaphragm opening size and the lens focal length. The length of the extension plus the lens original focal length becomes the new effective focal length. Thus, a 50 mm focal length lens set at f/8 will have an aperture diameter of 1/8 of 50 mm or 6.25 mm. Adding 50 mm extension tube length will change the "f-number" to f/16 (6.25/100).

Extension tubes normally are available in sets of three of varying lengths with a total length when combined of about 50 mm. Longer individual extension tubes are also available. Unless a double cable release is used the full aperture focusing with stopped down exposure feature of the modern SLR is lost. Exposures are taken in the camera's stopped down mode (this requires matching the exposure needle in the view finder to an index mark). Unless the extension tube set is specifically

| T Adapter | T-Flange | Extension Tubes | Variable Close-up Lens |

+1, +2, +4 Close-up Lens   +20, +10 Close-up Lens   Flat Field Lens 35, 75, 150mm

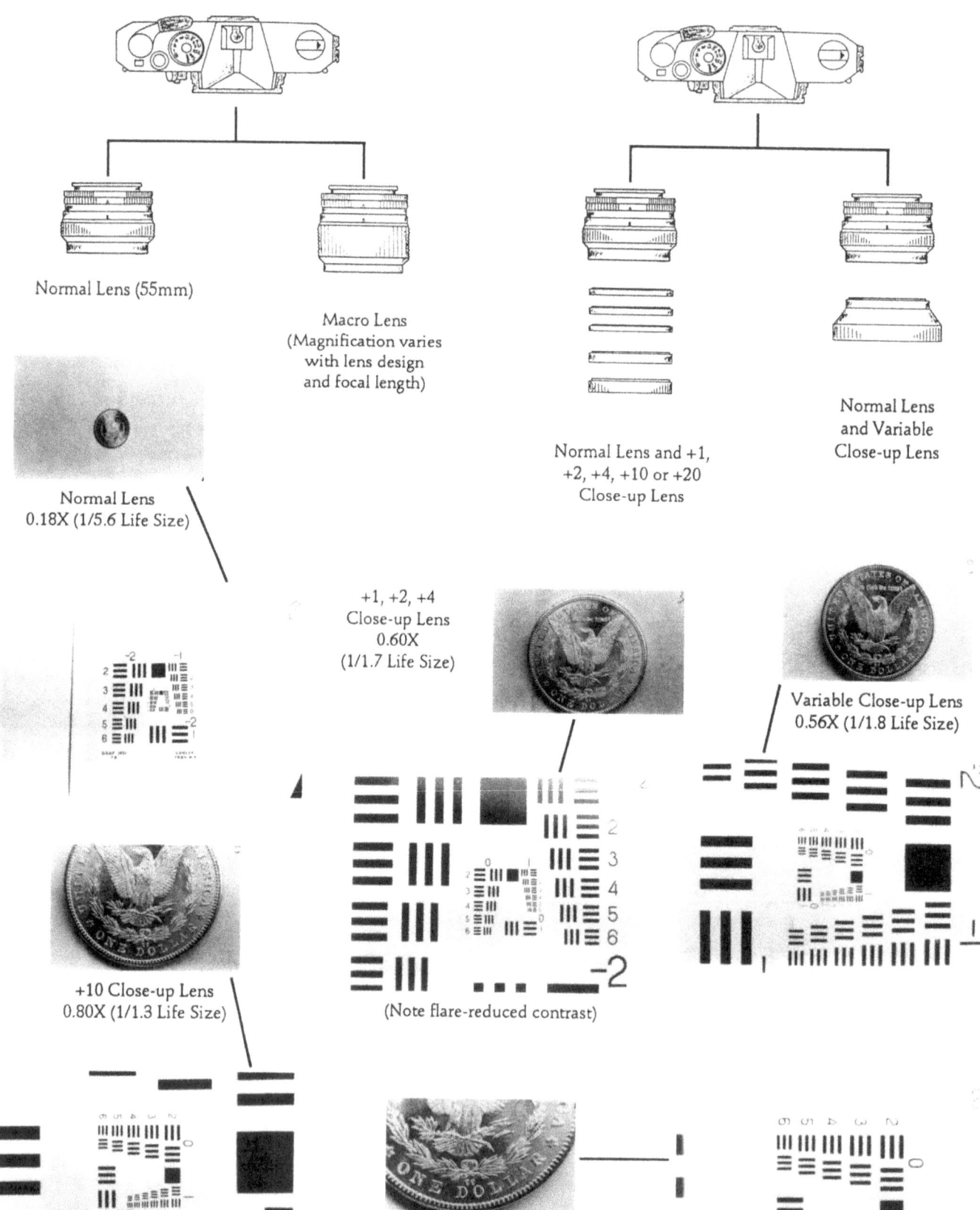

NORMAL CAMERA

SUPPLEMENTING NORMAL LENS

Normal Lens (55mm)

Macro Lens
(Magnification varies
with lens design
and focal length)

Normal Lens and +1,
+2, +4, +10 or +20
Close-up Lens

Normal Lens
and Variable
Close-up Lens

Normal Lens
0.18X (1/5.6 Life Size)

+1, +2, +4
Close-up Lens
0.60X
(1/1.7 Life Size)

Variable Close-up Lens
0.56X (1/1.8 Life Size)

+10 Close-up Lens
0.80X (1/1.3 Life Size)

(Note flare-reduced contrast)

+20 Close-up Lens
1.9X Life Size

(Note edge distortion)

(Note extreme distortion at edges)

made for a particular brand camera, a "T" adapter will be required to match the camera body to the extension tube set (usually a standard "T" mount size). A "T" flange will usually be required to match the extension tube to the camera lens (male "T" mount to equivalent camera body female mount fitting).

A bellows can be considered a variable extension tube. The disadvantage of an extension tube set is that the magnification obtained is governed by their fixed length which may not always match the photo needs. Bellows cost more than an extension tube set but are much more versatile. Some have a separate focusing rail to achieve focusing without changing the magnification. They also need a "T" flange and "T" adapter unless made specifically for the brand of camera. Double cable releases allow viewing at full aperture. Extension tubes can be used in conjunction with bellows to achieve even greater extension lengths and magnifications.

The accompanying photos show the magnification achieved with typical extension tubes and bellows. Extension tubes can achieve about 3 times life size on the 35 mm film negative. Bellows give up to about 6 times and the combination of the two give up to about 8 times life size. This is sufficient magnification for detailed blow-ups of individual Morgan dollar mint marks.

However, note that there is introduced some edge distortion at these extreme close-ups. This is because the normal camera lens was designed to give best resolution when focused at infinity. They were not designed to give best performance when the distance to the subject (coin) is less than the effective focal length (or about 1:1 reproduction ratio).

Reversing Normal Lens

Most camera manufacturers recommend reversing the normal camera lens if reproduction ratios of greater than 1:1 are to be used. This changes the geometry of the optics back to the designed relationships of greater distance for the lens front than the rear. In addition to giving better sharpness and resolution, the focusing field is flatter, better matching the flat coin surface.

Instead of using a "T" flange to attach the normal camera lens to the extension tubes and bellows, a reversing ring adapter is used. Other than that change, the same extension tubes and bellows and their combinations can be used as for extending the normal lens as previously discussed.

The accompanying photos show the magnification and definition achieved using the normal camera lens in the reversed position. Without extension tubes or bellows, the reversed lens can give magnification of about ½ life size. However, note that there is quite a bit of edge distortion. This is due to the front of the lens being closer to the film plane than the lens rear to the subject, in contradiction to the intent of the lens design.

The normal lens in the reversed position should be used only with extension tubes or bellows in order to give good resolution and definition across the entire film frame width. Extension tubes can give about 3 times magnification using the typical set of three. Bellows can give about 6 times magnification and their combination about 8 times. The definition is quite good even at the frame edges.

Camera Body, T Adapter, Extension Tubes, Normal Lens

Camera Body, T Adapter, Extension Tubes, Reverse Ring, Normal Lens (Reversed)

Camera Body, T Adapter, Extension Tubes, Flat Field Lens

EXTENDING NORMAL LENS

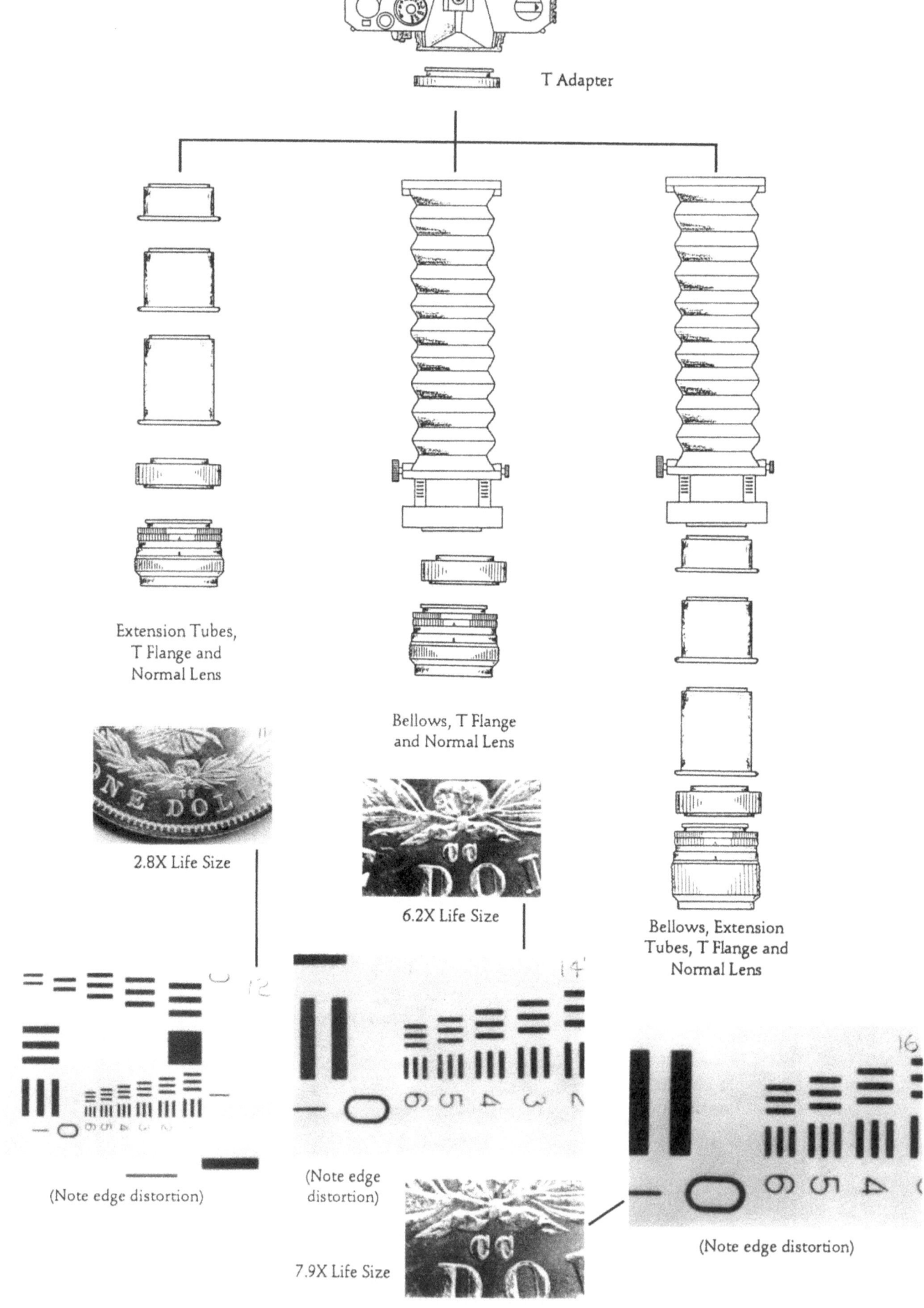

T Adapter

Extension Tubes,
T Flange and
Normal Lens

2.8X Life Size

(Note edge distortion)

Bellows, T Flange
and Normal Lens

6.2X Life Size

(Note edge
distortion)

7.9X Life Size

Bellows, Extension
Tubes, T Flange and
Normal Lens

(Note edge distortion)

REVERSING NORMAL LENS

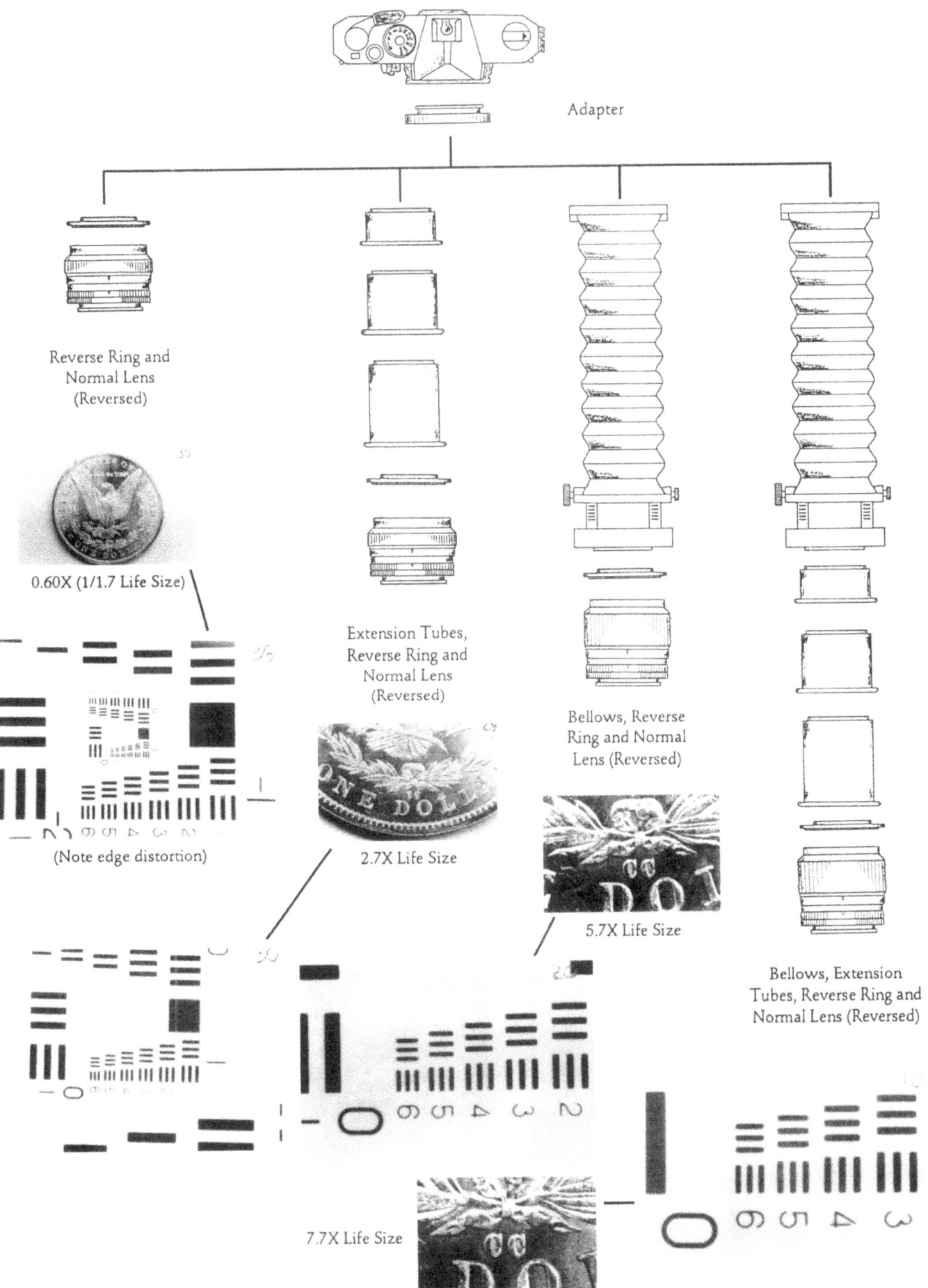

Adapter

Reverse Ring and
Normal Lens
(Reversed)

0.60X (1/1.7 Life Size)

(Note edge distortion)

Extension Tubes,
Reverse Ring and
Normal Lens
(Reversed)

2.7X Life Size

Bellows, Reverse
Ring and Normal
Lens (Reversed)

5.7X Life Size

Bellows, Extension
Tubes, Reverse Ring and
Normal Lens (Reversed)

7.7X Life Size

Special Flat Field Lens

Flat field lens are designed to photograph flat subjects such as coins. Thus, they are better suited to take whole coins or extreme close-ups of mint marks than even the reversed normal lens. Flat field lens are available in a variety of focal lengths at modest cost compared to most SLR camera lens. They normally do not have a focusing capability and do not have very fast lens. The average enlarger lens is a good example of a flat field lens and they can be obtained for as low as about $20.

The accompanying photos show the magnification and definition obtained with an enlarger lens of 35 mm focal length. Using the lens without extension gives a magnification of ½. Various combinations of extension tubes and bellows can give magnification of up to 12 times. This can provide really large blow-ups of just the mint mark of the Morgan dollar. With a flat field capability, these lens provide good definition from edge to edge of the film frame.

Special 2X Converter

An interesting supplementary lens is the 2x T-converter. It is used in conjunction with extension tubes and/or bellows to provide an increased magnification. A side benefit is that it also enables the reversed normal lens or flat field lens to be further away from the subject (coin). This allows greater freedom in providing direct lighting over the coin. However, it does introduce some edge distortion.

MICROSCOPES

Even greater magnification can be achieved by using the SLR camera with microscopes. A "T" adapter is required along with a microscope adapter. Magnifications of 25 time or greater can be achieved. However, as the magnifications become greater, the depth of field becomes less so that the entire mint mark cannot be in focus at the same time. Either the top surface or the surrounding field can only be in focus.

Using the SLR with a stereo microscope can be convenient since as the coins are examined, any points of interest can be easily photographed. The greater depth of field and wider angle of the stereo microscope than the usual mono microscope makes it more suitable for coin photography.

SETTING UP THE CAMERA

Typically, the SLR camera in combination with a bellows and normal lens or a flat field lens is mounted on a copy stand. This gives a convenient method to raise and lower the whole combination over a flat surface onto which to place the coin. A tripod can also be used to mount the combination but it must be angled over the edge of a table and it is more difficult to raise and lower.

A "T" adapter is used to attach the camera body (either bayonet or threaded) to the threaded top of the bellows extension. A dual track bellow extension is preferable for stability and it should have a locking knob to secure the end of the bellows to the track. A separate focusing track where the bellows extension attaches to the copy stand allows focusing without changing the magnification but it is not necessary. A reverse ring adapter connects the outside of the camera lens to the end of the bellows. The camera lens attaches to the bellows in the reverse position. A normal focal length camera lens of about 50 mm is used. Most flat field lens will fit directly onto the bellows or extension tubes without ring adapters. The cable release is necessary to take vibration free shots.

The coin is laid on a protective cloth on the copy stand base or near the edge of a table if a tripod is used. The camera film plane must be parallel to the coin surface to prevent distortion.

If only some portion of the coin is to be photographed then the color of the background cloth or paper does not matter. Photographs of the full coin will show the background. For publications, usually only the coin is to be shown so a white background is used for black and white prints or just the coin is cut out of the print. A black background is sometimes used to sharpen the coin contrast (by reducing the flare in the camera lens) or to make a silver coin stand out more. For color slides or prints, a harmonizing or contrasting color background is used.

Plastic holders are available to hold the coin on its edge to take photographs of railroad rims. Special holders are also available or can be made with two mirrors at right angles to photograph coins with rotated reverses. In this case, the coin is placed on its edge between the vee formed by the two mirrors. The negative must be placed upside down in the enlarger to show the proper left-right relationship in the print for the rotated reverse taken with mirrors.

TAKING THE PICTURE

Before the coin is placed under the camera for close-up photographs, it should first be examined with a hand held magnifying glass to fix in one's mind the exact features to be captured in the photographs. The type and extent of doubling, orientation of the mint mark and date, or other feature details should be checked so it can later be detected through the camera view finder as the coin orientation and lighting is adjusted.

Next, the coin is placed under the camera in the approximate position for taking the picture. The camera lens "f stop" is adjusted to obtain a fairly bright image, usually about f/4 or /5.6. Then the copy stand height and bellows extension position is adjusted to bring the coin into focus on the ground glass or other type focusing screen in the SLR camera view finder. The coin is moved until the portion of the coin to be photographed comes

SPECIAL FLAT FIELD LENS

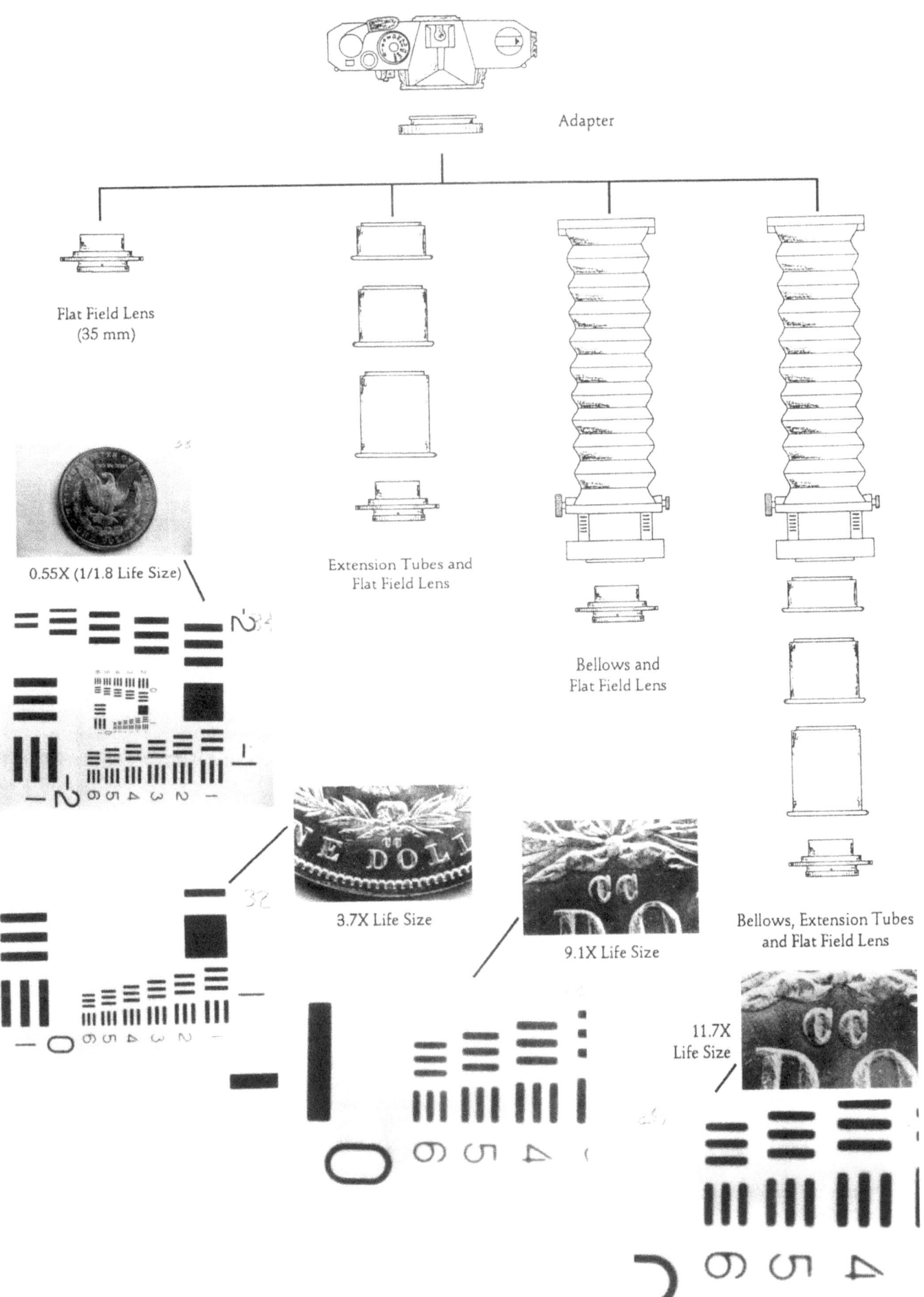

Adapter

Flat Field Lens
(35 mm)

0.55X (1/1.8 Life Size)

Extension Tubes and
Flat Field Lens

Bellows and
Flat Field Lens

Bellows, Extension Tubes
and Flat Field Lens

3.7X Life Size

9.1X Life Size

11.7X
Life Size

PHOTOMICROGRAPHY

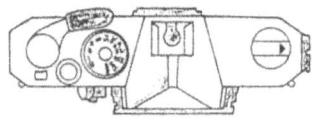

Camera Body

Adapter

Microscope
Adapter

7.7X Life Size
(With bellows, reverse ring and
normal lens reversed)

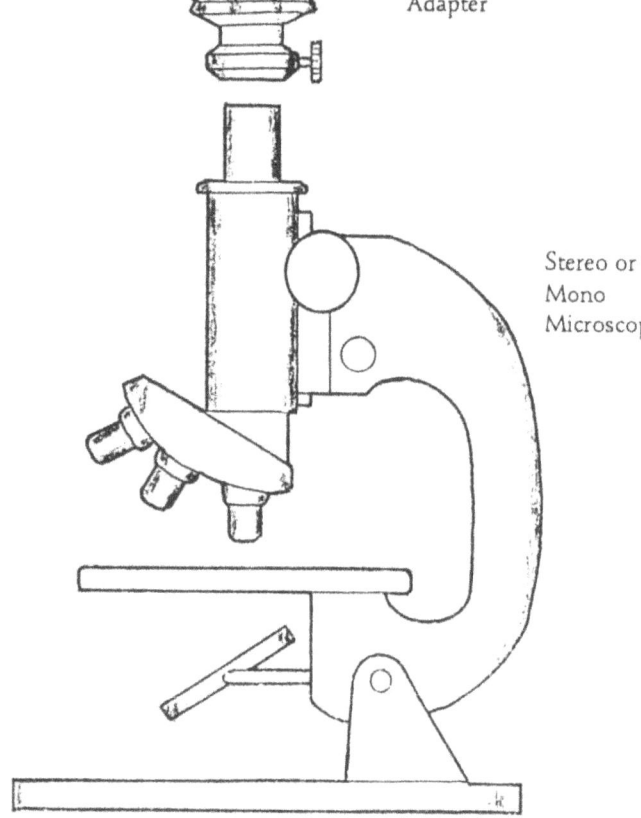

Stereo or
Mono
Microscope

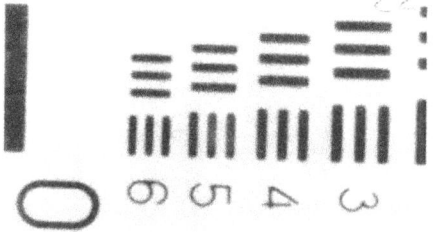

(Note some edge distortion)

2X T-Converter

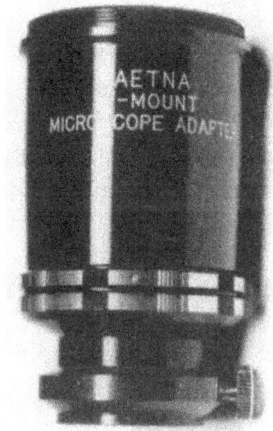

Microscope Adapter

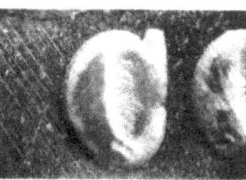

26X Life Size

(Note ex-
tremely shal-
low depth of
field – top of
mint mark
out of focus)

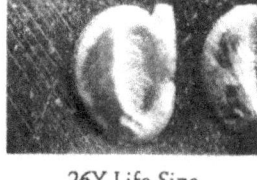

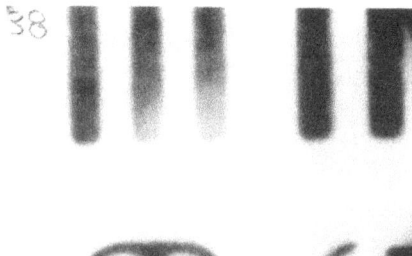

Camera Body, T-Adapter, Bellows, Extension Tubes, Flat Field Lens

Camera with Bellows on Copy Stand

Camera and Bellows Extension
Left to right: SLR 35mm Camera Body, T-Adapter, Bellows Extension, Ring Adapter,
Camera Lens (Reversed); Bottom: Cable Release

into view. An advantage of the SLR 35 mm camera is that the view finder shows exactly what will be taken by the film. Since focusing is also accomplished on the picture image coming through the camera lens, focusing is relatively easy.

Usually on the first try the coin image will not be of proper size. Either not all of the desired portion of the coin will be shown or it will be within only a small portion of the view-finder. The objective is to have the feature to be photographed cover most of the view-finder area and include some surrounding details to aid in the orientation or placement on the coin. The extension of the bellows and the copy stand height (or separate bellows camera track if available) are alternately adjusted until the desired portion of the coin fills the view-finder and is in focus. The bellows and copy stand are now locked in this position.

If photographs of the complete silver dollar are desired, several methods can be used. A normal camera lens in combination with a variable close-up supplemental lens will produce good results. A macro lens is most convenient with a wide range of focusing distance and yields excellent photographs. The normal camera lens can be reversed but is not recommended because of edge distortion introduced. Extension tubes can be used with the normal camera lens as long as the extension tube is not more than about half the lens focal length. Alternately, an inexpensive flat-field (enlarger) lens can be used. A 35 mm flat-field lens will allow about 0.5 life-size negatives but with a fixed focus it will provide only one size and the camera body must be moved to achieve correct focus on the coin. A longer focal length flat-field lens of 50 mm or 75 mm can be used with bellows to allow easier focusing.

A critical phase of photographing coins is adjusting the lighting. It is assumed that the coins have been cleaned if necessary. The lighting must now be adjusted to bring out the details desired; overall coin design, doubled details, or special details. This can be a very frustrating and time consuming job; and if it is not done properly a very unsatisfactory photograph will be produced even though the focusing and exposure were correct.

The light source is first placed near the bellows up high to give direct vertical lighting. This produces an even light over all the coin surface without shadows or strong reflected light spots. Usually this position will produce the best lighting results. The light source should be varied around the camera and in height and lateral position until the optimum combination is found. Doubled letters and designs are best shown with nearly vertical lighting to eliminate the strong shadows and bright spots.

The camera lens is now stepped down to f-8 or f-11. This increases the depth of the field so that all of the coin is in focus from the center to the edge of the frame and from the coin field to the tops of the coin design. In addition, the camera lens resolution is usually best in the range of f-5.6 to f-11.

Finally, the camera shutter speed must be set for the correct film exposure. Films such as Kodak Plus X for general purpose medium size prints and Kodak Pantatomic-X for extreme size enlargements produce satisfactory results. With film speed ratings of ASA 125 and 64, respectively, the exposure times for close-up pictures will be about ¼ to 1 second. The modem SLR 35 mm camera with built-in through the lens exposure metering system makes getting the correct film exposure for every frame very easy. Depending on the brand camera, the metering needle or indicator is set to the stopped down mark. Consult your particular camera manual on instructions for obtaining correct exposures for manual or stopped down exposure operation. To achieve the correct exposure indication, the shutter speed is adjusted in combination with the aperture setting (f-5.6 to f-11 in one half stops).

Colored 35 mm slides or prints of your coins can also be easily made with the SLR 35 mm camera. If outdoor film is used then it is best to take the photographs outdoors in direct sunlight. Filters are available to convert outdoor film to indoor lighting but the film speed is reduced by a factor of 2 to 3. This requires very long exposure times with most types of indoor lighting which may be outside the range of some camera metering systems.

A record of each exposure should be made by identifying the frame number, particular coin, and the detail of interest. The camera aperture and shutter setting may also want to be recorded; especially for the first few rolls of film shot of the coins. This allows a later appraisal of the correctness of the exposure and corrections to be made in subsequent rolls of film.

Use of camera types other than the SLR is much more difficult. The range finder type cameras have focusing indicators and metering systems that are separate from the camera lens. With close-up lens attached to the normal camera lens, focusing can be achieved by setting the camera lens to coin distance recommended for the particular close-up lens used. Alternatively, the back of the camera can be opened (before loading the film) and a piece of ground glass or waxed paper placed at the normal film very position. Then, with the shutter open in the time setting, the focusing adjustment can be made. The external exposure metering system will give an approximate exposure

setting. This setting should be bracketed by higher and lower exposure settings for the first few rolls until the metering system suitability is established.

Modern twin lens reflex camera can also be used with close-up lens to take pictures of coins. Extreme close-up photographs with this type camera or the range finder type camera are not generally possible. The coin is placed under the viewing lens, with the camera set exactly parallel to the surface supporting the coin. With the close-up lens attached to the viewing lens, the camera focus and distance to the coin are adjusted to make the ground glass image sharp. If the camera had a built in exposure system, then it can be used to set the camera exposure. The coin is then centered in front of the main camera lens and the close-up lens attached to this lens.

PROCESSING THE FILM

The simplest way for film processing is to have it developed and prints made by a commercial firm. Alternatively, the film can be easily developed at home to save processing costs, obtain the developed film quicker, or to ensure consistently good results.

For film development at home all that is needed is a light tight roll film developing tank plus the developer, stop bath, and fixer solutions. All these items are inexpensive. A fine grain developer such as Microdol should be used, following the manufacturer's instructions. The film can be loaded into the developing tank in a closet or a closed room at night if a photographic dark room is not available.

If only a few frames of a roll have been exposed, then this part of a roll can be cut off in a suitable darkened room for immediate development at home. The end of the remaining unexposed portion of the film can be rethreaded into the camera's take-up spool after the leading edge is cut in half with scissors to form a leader. If many pictures of coins are to be made, it is usually cheaper to buy the film in bulk cans and load your own rolls.

MAKING YOUR OWN PRINTS

With access to a photographic enlarger, prints of the coins can also be made quite easily. Standard printing procedures and chemicals are used. A glossy white paper will give the best definition, but other textures can be used to suit one's preference. Single weight paper is satisfactory for most applications. If the print is to be published, a glossy white paper is preferred. Double weight paper minimizes the curling of the print edges, but single weight RC (resin coated) paper is acceptable nowadays for most publications.

The contrast of coins is very low since there is not the change of materials or reflectance found in the normal camera subjects. Thus, best prints are obtained if a slightly contrasting paper is used, about No. 3 paper.

This will show greater tone variation across the coin making the details more noticeable. If the print is to be published however, a slightly light print is desirable since the publishing process usually darkens the picture.

The record of the exposures taken for the roll being printed will have to be referred to in the darkroom. Most of the time, only a portion of the frame will need to be printed. Therefore, one must know what portion of the date or other coin area to print by referring to the exposure record and noting the detail of interest.

One standard darkroom technique that can be very useful in making coin prints is dodging. Often times, the lighting may not be even across the whole coin surface. This can be easily corrected in the printing process by dodging in the darker areas to lighten them (by interposing one's hand briefly over the photographic paper to block excess light in a particular area).

1878 P

14-11 $I^1 11 \cdot A^1 c$ (Doubled Eyelid) (189?) I-3 R-7

Obverse $I^1 11$– Eyelid doubled as short, thick and blunt spike just below eyelid plus a long thin spike angled downward in front of lower part of eye. E and P of E PLURIBUS doubled in clockwise direction. Raised metal in first 8 in date. Ear over polished. Strong doubling along top edges of many obverse stars.

14-12 $I^1 12 \cdot A^1 c$ (Doubled Date) (189?) I-3 R-7

Obverse $I^1 12$– Thin spike below eyelid. Slightly doubled date. 1 doubled below upper crossbar, first 8 doubled at top inside of both loops and bottom left outside of upper loop, 7 doubled below crossbar and right side of vertical shaft, second 8 doubled at top inside and bottom left outside of upper loop.
Reverse $A^1 c$– Die further polished down.

14-13 $I^1 13 \cdot A^1 n$ (Bar Eyelid) (189) I-3 R-7

Obverse $I^1 13$– Extra metal in front of eye as thick bar just below front of eyelid. Date tripled with 1 slightly tripled at lower left outside and top inside of upper loop. 7 slightly tripled below crossbar and doubled at top right. Second 8 slightly tripled at lower left outside of upper loop. All right stars very slightly doubled towards rim.

14-14 $I^1 14 \cdot A^1 c$ (Doubled LIBERTY) (189) I-3 R-7

Obverse $I^1 14$– Slightly doubled LIBERTY on right side, E PLURIB at top outside, tops of cotton leaves, bottom of nostril and nose and right side of 7. All left stars doubled towards rim and first 3 right stars tripled and 4-6 right stars doubled towards rim. Spike below eyelid and small die chip in front of lower eye. Horizontal and vertical die cracks through second 8.

14-15 $I^1 2 \cdot A^1 l$ (Doubled Motto) (193) I-3 R-7

199-1 $II/I\ 17 \cdot B^2 f$ (Tripled Cotton Bolls) (194) I-3 R-6

1878 S

26 $II\ 23 \cdot B^1 a$ (Long Center Arrow Shaft, S Tilted Left) (186) I-3 R-7

Obverse II 23– Eyelid doubled at bottom front and short spikes at eye bottom front and lower part of eye socket.
Reverse $B^1 a$– Normal die of 1878 P B1 type with long center arrow shaft. Small III S mint mark set slightly to right with slight tilt to left.

27 $II\ 1 \cdot B^1 b$ (Long Center Arrow Shaft) (185) I-3 R-7

Reverse $B^1 b$– Small III S mint mark centered and upright.

56 $II\ 24 \cdot B^1 c$ (Long Center Arrow Shaft, S Set High) (184) I-3 R-7

Obverse II 24– Two horizontal bars out from front of eye. L of LIBERTY slightly doubled on lower left serif.
Reverse $B^1 c$– Small III S mint mark set high, slightly to left and upright.

57 $II\ 23 \cdot B^1 d$ (Long Center Arrow Shaft, S Set Left) (?) I-3 R-7

Reverse $B^1 d$– Small III S mint mark set slightly left well below wreath, with slight tilt to left. Die chip in G of GOD.

58   II 25 • B^{1}c (Long Center Arrow Shaft, S Set High)   (?)   I-3   R-7

Obverse II 25– Thick spike just below eyelid in front of eye. Slight doubling inside inner ear.

1879 O

28   III^{2}20 • C^{3}c (O/O Horizontal, Doubled 87)   (176)   I-3   R-6

Obverse III^{2}20– Doubled 87 in date, 8 doubled on lower outside of lower loop. 7 strongly doubled on entire right side of vertical stem.

1880 O

45   III^{2}19 • C^{3}j (Doubled 80, O/O Left)   (176)   I-2   R-3

Reverse C^{3}j– II O mint mark doubled at bottom inside as curved line with polishing marks just above it, long thin diagonal line at lower left outside and short arc line at top outside.

46   III^{2}34 • C^{3}a (Doubled Ear, Motto and 80)   (176)   I-3   R-3

Obverse III^{2}34– Ear doubled slightly on right side of inner ear fill and outside. Motto letters and 5 and 6 right stars doubled slightly towards rim. Second 8 doubled slightly at lower left outside of upper loop. 0 doubled slightly at left inside and right outside. Pitted die below 88.

47   III^{2}35 • C^{3}a (Doubled Motto, 88)   (176)   I-2   R-3

Obverse III^{2}35– Motto letters doubled slightly at top towards rim. First 8 doubled slightly on right inside of lower loop. Second 8 doubled slightly at lower left outside of upper loop.

1881 O

27   III^{2}16 • C^{3}a (Doubled Ear)   (176)   I-3   R-7

Obverse III^{2}16– Doubled back and base of ear, front inside of ear and hair above ear. LIBERTY slightly doubled on right side.

1882 O

35   III^{2}10 • C^{3}h (Metal in 882, O/O Lower left)   (181)   I-2   R-4

Obverse III^{2}10– Die flakes in 882 openings. 18 not doubled, thus previous die listing could be machine doubling.

36   III^{2}26 • C^{3}h (Doubled 82, O/O Center)   (?)   I-2   R-5

Obverse III^{2}26– Doubled 82 in date. Second 8 doubled at left outside of both loops. 2 doubled at top and right outside of upper loop. Closed 2. Raised dots on Liberty Head from rusted die.

Reverse C^{3}m– II O mint mark repunched with original showing as thin vertical lines on left and right sides of opening. Raised dots on eagle from rusted die.

1884 O

37   III^{2}14 • C^{3}a (Date in Denticles)   (181)   I-4   R-3

Obverse III^{2}14– Date mispunched low in denticles showing as three small raised bars below 18 and 88 in denticles spaces.

38   III^{2}15 • C^{3}a (Possible ES in Denticles)   (181)   I-4   R-3

Obverse III^{2}15– Raised curved line in denticle space below first 8 and raised curved bar with straight top below second 8. Possible ES in STATES from reverse hub impressed in denticle spacing below 88. Perhaps used to position second 8 of date on vertical center line above E impression.

1885 P

1C   III²1 • C³a (Pitted Reverse)   (188)   I-2   R-6
Reverse C³a– Die is slightly pitted on upper leaves of wreath to left of ribbon bow and in field below arrowheads.

1887 O

23   III²19 • C³a (Quadrupled Stars, Near Date)   (181)   I-3   R-6
Obverse III²19– All left stars tripled or quadrupled towards rim and all right stars doubled towards rim. Date set further left than normal.

24   III²20 • C³a (Doubled Eyelid and Ear)   (181)   I-3   R-4
Obverse III²20– Right inside of ear strongly doubled. Slight doubling of lower front of eyelid, hair strands just to right of ear and lower cotton leaf left side.

1888 P

20   III²16 • C³a (Doubled Profile)   (190)   I-3   R-3
Obverse III²16– Doubled Liberty's profile, bottom of eyelid, bottom outside of earlobe and lower cotton leaf left side.

21   III²17 • C³a (Doubled Ear)   (190)   I-2   R-3
Obverse III²17– Doubled right inside of ear.

1888 O

18   III²12 • C³b (Doubled 88, Oval O)   (181)   I-3   R-4
Obverse III²12– First 8 in date doubled very slightly at bottom outside. Second 8 doubled at bottom outside.

1889 P

19A   III²1 • C³b (Bar Wing)   (190)   I-3   R-6
Reverse C³b– Die break on top of eagle's right wing showing as a short parallel bar.

22   III²5 • C³b (Bar Wing, Far Date)   (190)   I-3   R-6
Reverse C³b– Later die state with die break on top of eagle's right wing showing as a short parallel bar.

23   III²21 • C³a (Slanted Date)   (190)   I-2   R-3
Obverse III²21– Date slanted with 9 higher than 1 and date in normal lateral position. Open 9.

23A   III²21 • C³a (Slanted Date, IN on Obverse)   (190)   I-5   R-7
Obverse III²21– Very strong die clashes with bottom of I and full N of IN GOD from reverse showing in front of Liberty's neck. Unique die clash of reverse lettering transfer to obverse.

1890 O

20   III²9 • C³a (Doubled Ear and Cotton Leaves)   (181)   I-3   R-5
Obverse III²9– Ear strongly doubled at bottom and halfway up side. Hair strongly doubled just above ear. Lower cotton leaves doubled on left side.

1891 O

1B   III²1 • C³a (Pitted Reverse)   (181)   I-2   R-6

Reverse C³a– Die is pitted on lower left of wreath extending down to E on ONE and from N of ONE down into denticles.

1896 P

19   III²19 • C³a (8 in Denticles)   (190)   I-3   R-5

Obverse III²19– Top of 8 appears in two denticle spaces just below 8 as two raised and curved bars.

1899 O

30   III²18 • C³b (Doubled 189, High O Tilted Right)   (?)   I-2   R-5

Obverse III²18– Doubled 189 in date. 1 is doubled slightly at bottom. 8 is doubled as thin lines well separated from right outside of upper loop and bottom right and right outside of lower loop. 9 is doubled as short thin vertical line in middle of upper loop.

1900 P

24   III²19 • C⁴/C³a (Doubled Eagle, Quintupled Stars)   (189)   I-4   R-5

Obverse III²19– All right stars and 1 and 2 left stars very slightly quintupled towards rim. Remainder of left stars doubled and tripled as are tops of NUM.

1901 P

11   III²5 • C⁴/C³? (Doubled Hair Above Ear)   (189)   I-3   R-5

Obverse III²5– Hair above ear doubled as well as forehead and profile with slight spike below eyelid.

1903 O

12   III²6 • C⁴g (O/O Down)   (?)   I-3   R-3

Obverse III²6– Very slightly doubled nose, lips and chin of Liberty head profile. Closed 9.

Reverse C⁴g– III O mint mark repunched with original showing as a thin curved line at lower left outside and slight short horizontal line next to top right outside.

1922 P

2G   II 1 • B²a (Scar Cheek)   I-3   R-6

Obverse II 1– Vertical die break and large die chip just behind Liberty's mouth.

6   II 1 • B²d (Doubled Reverse)   I-3   R-3

Reverse B²d– Doubled bottom of olive leaves, berries and stems, back of leg feathers, lower rays, base of DOLLAR and E of E PLURIBUS.

7   II 1 • B²e (Doubled Wing)   I-3   R-3

Reverse B²e– Strong doubling on eagle's right wing and down right edge and slightly doubled stems and bottoms of top olive leaves.

1922 D

4   II 2 • B²c (Doubled TRUST)   I-3   R-3

Obverse II 2– TRUST, de Francisci's monogram and date doubled towards rim with slight doubling along bottom of neck and WE.

Reverse B²c– Doubled bottom edge of right leaves, left edge of eagle's left leg feathers and rays below leg feathers.

1922 S

3   II 1 • B²b (Tripled Reverse)   I-3   R-3

Reverse B²b– Tripled front edge of eagle's right wing, doubled top of eagle's head, top inside of upper beak, throat and right edge of neck feathers, tripled rays below, thru and above ONE, doubled back of leg feathers, slightly doubled right side of rays thru DOLLAR, slightly tripled lower olive leaves and doubled top olive leaf on left side.

1925 S

3   II 1 • B²c (Doubled Wing)   I-3   R-3

Reverse B²c– Doubled outside edge of eagle's right wing from shoulder down to right talon, bottoms of eagle's right leg feathers and bottom edges of top olive leaves.

1926 P

3   II 2 • B²c (Doubled 6)   I-3   R-3

Obverse II 2– Doubled tip of 6 in date, designer's initial and T in TRUST.

1878 P 14-11 O I^{1}11

1878 P   14-12 O II ^{1}2

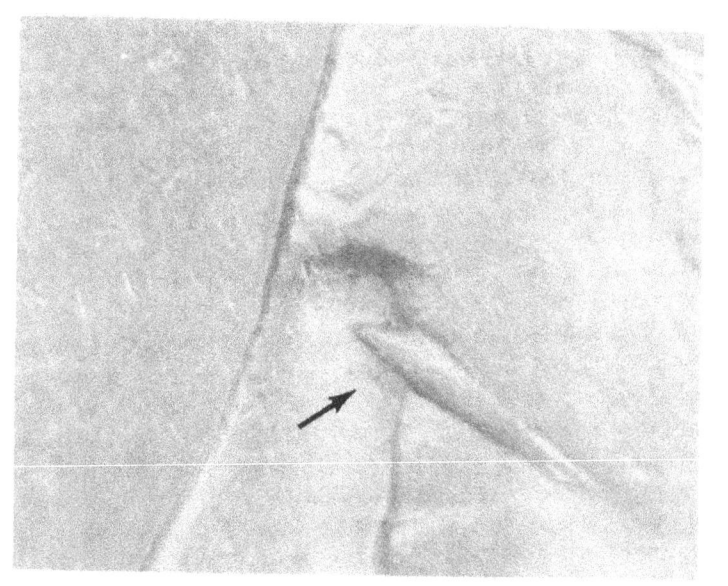

1878 P   14-13 O I^1 13

1878 P   14-14 O   I^1 14

1878 S 26 O II 23

1878 S 56 O II 24

1878 S 56 R B^{1}c

1878 S 57 R B^{1}d

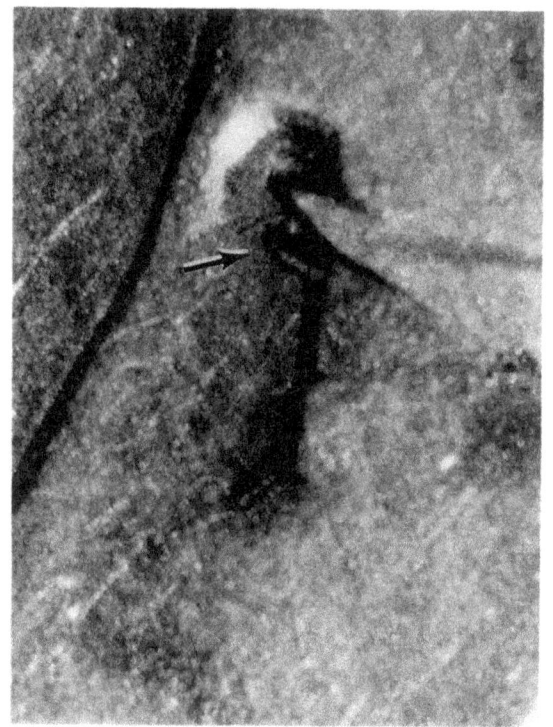

1878 S 58 O   II 25

1879 O
Doubled 87
28 O   III^2 20

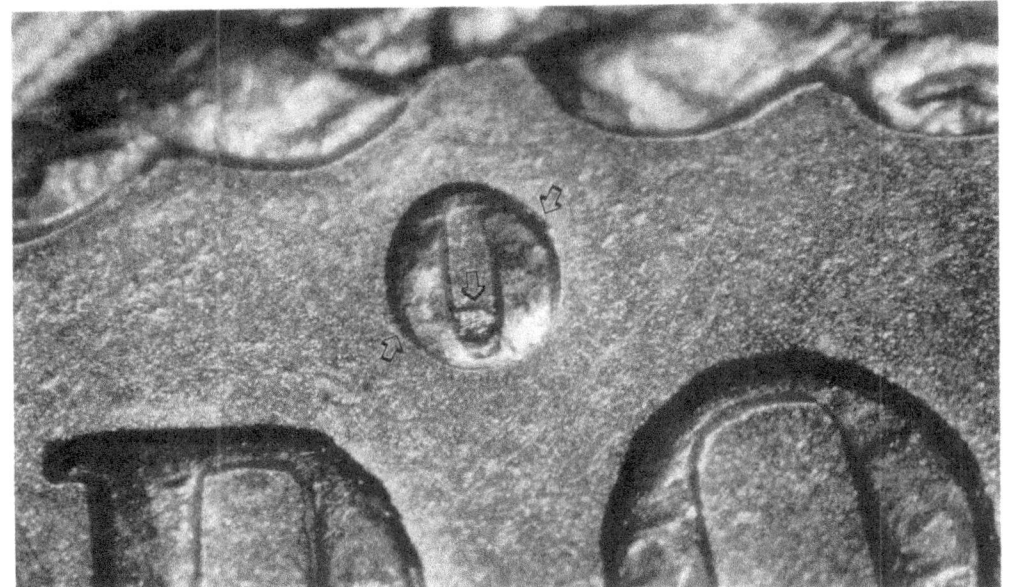

1880 O
O/O Left
45 R $C^{-3}j$

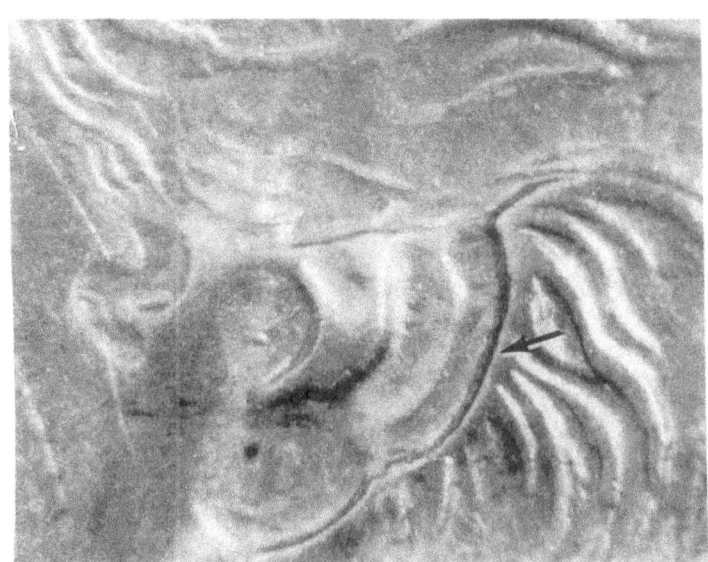

1880 Doubled ear
46 O III^2 34

1880 O
Doubled motto, 88
47 O III^2 35

1881 O
Doubled ear
27 O III^2 16

1882 O
Dobuled 82
36 O III^{2}26

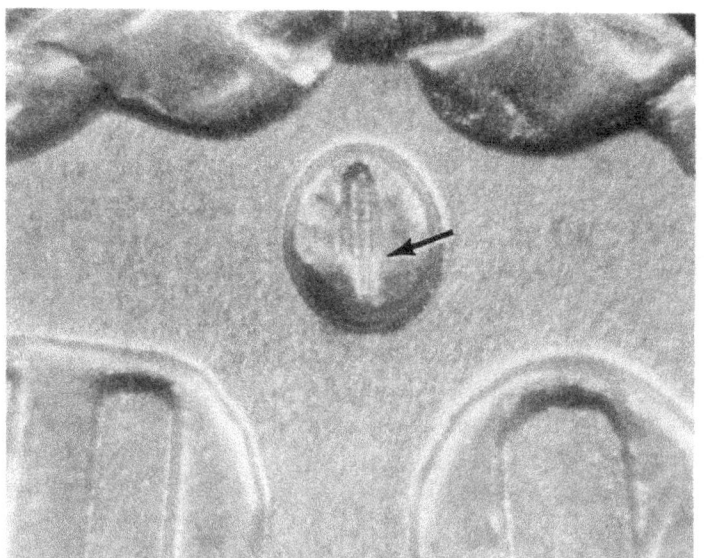

1882 O
O/O Center
36 R C^{3}h

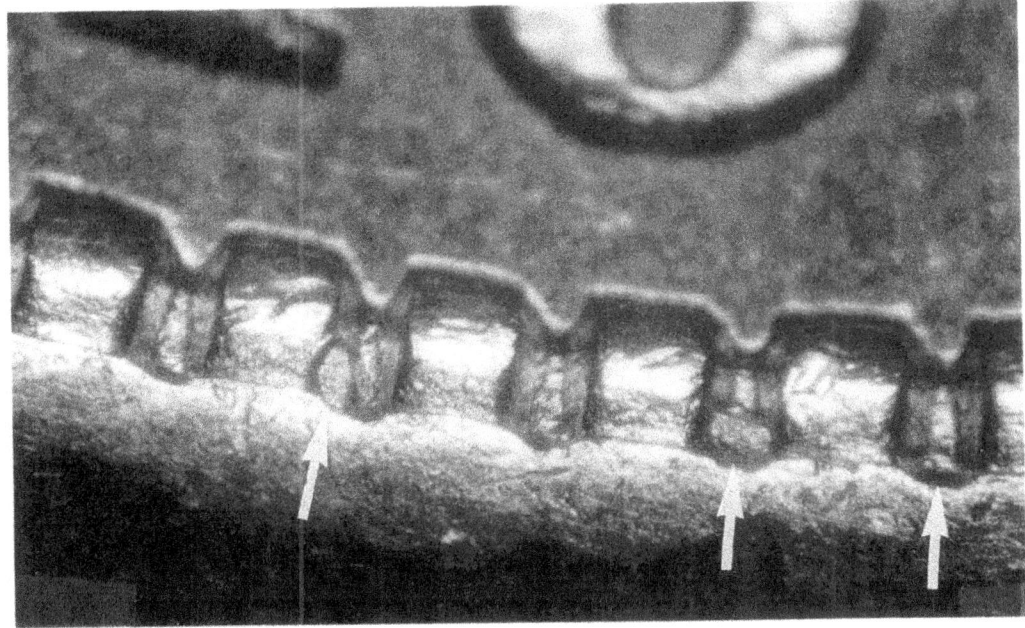

1884 O
Date in denticles
37 O   III[2] 14

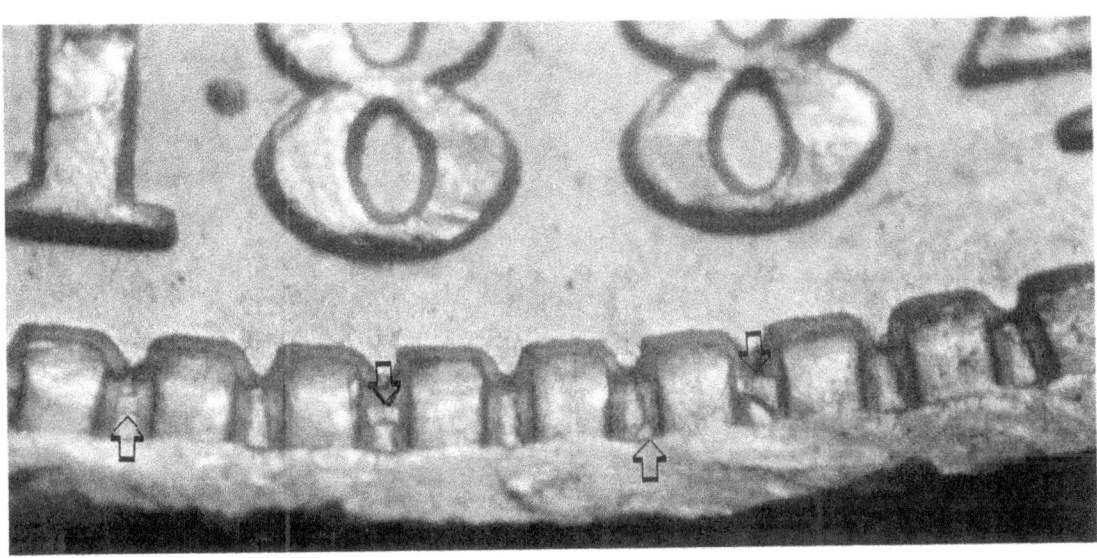

1884 O
ES in Denticles
38 O   III[2]15

1885 P
Pitted Reverse
1C R   C[3]a

1887 O
Doubled ear
24 O III^2 20

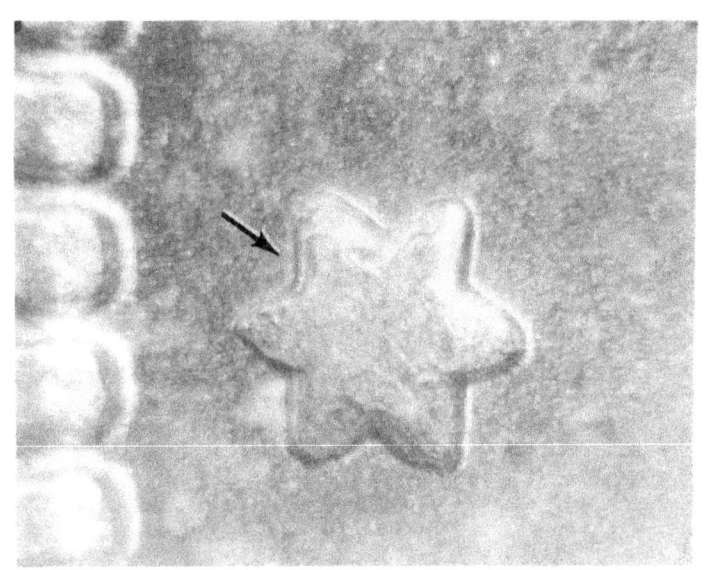

1887 O
Quadrupled stars
23 O III^{2}19

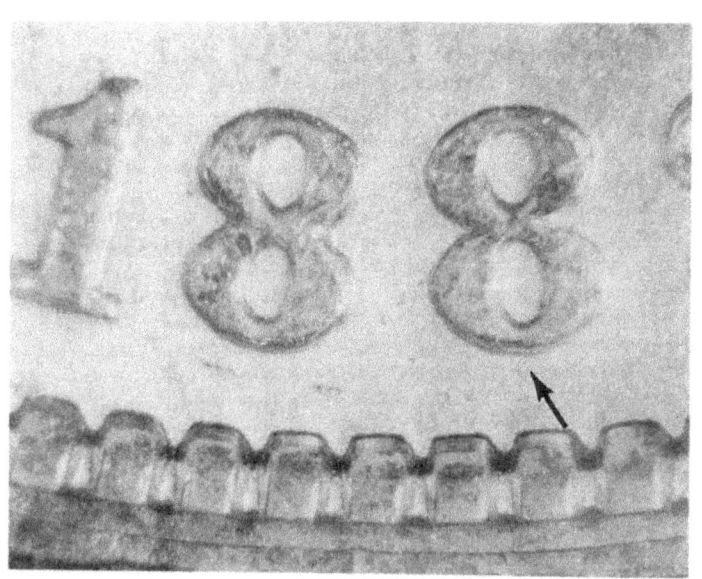

1888 O
Doubled 88
18 O III ^{2}12

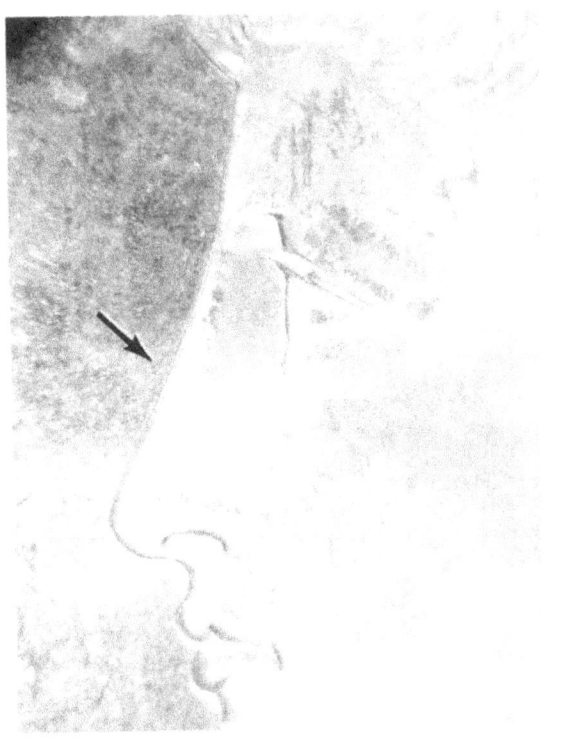

1888 P
Doubled Profile
20 O III^2 16

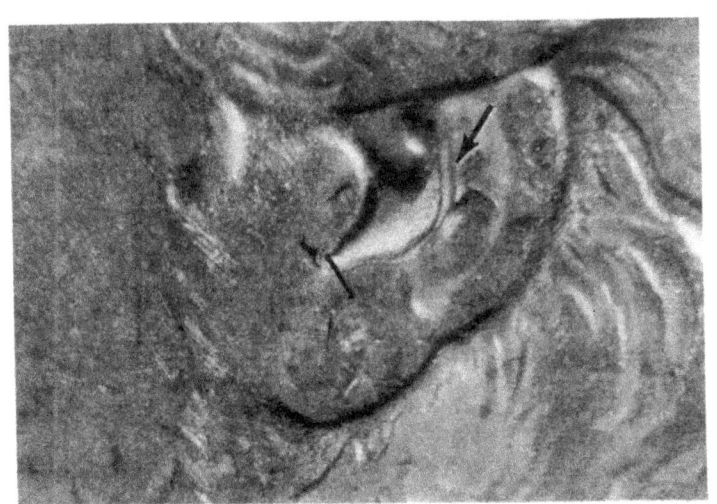

1888 P
Doubled ear
21 O   III^{2}17

1889 P
Slanted date
23 O III ^{2}21

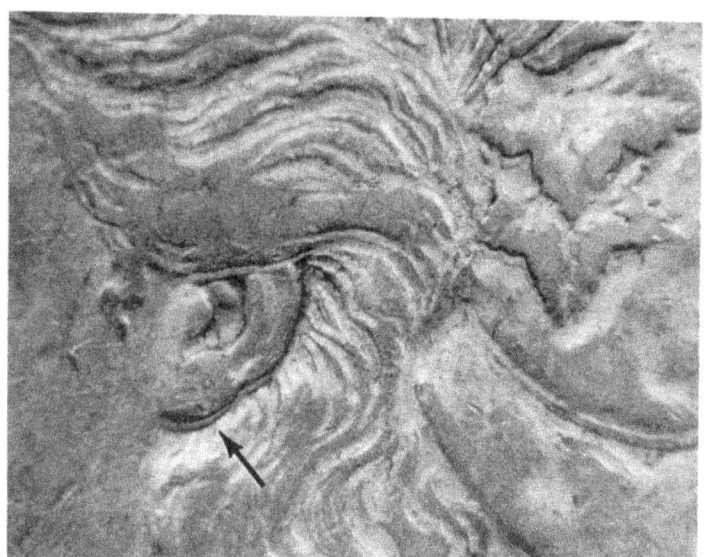

1889 P
In on Obverse
23 A O III^2 21

1890 O
Doubled ear
20 O III^2 9

1891 O
Pitted Reverse
1 B O III^2 1

1896 P
8 In Denticles
19 O III^2 19

1899 O
Doubled 189
30 O III^2 18

1903 O
O/O Down
12 R C^4 g

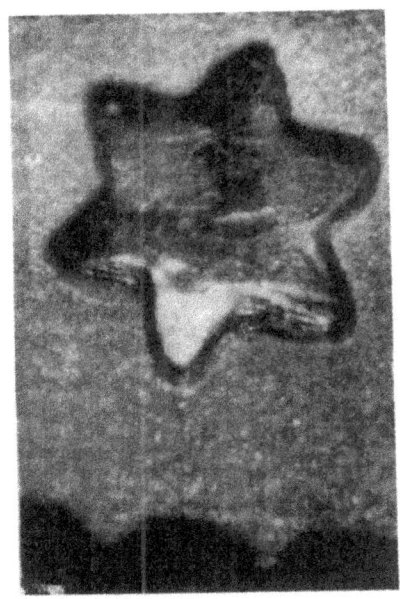

1900 P
Quintupled stars
24 O III^2 19

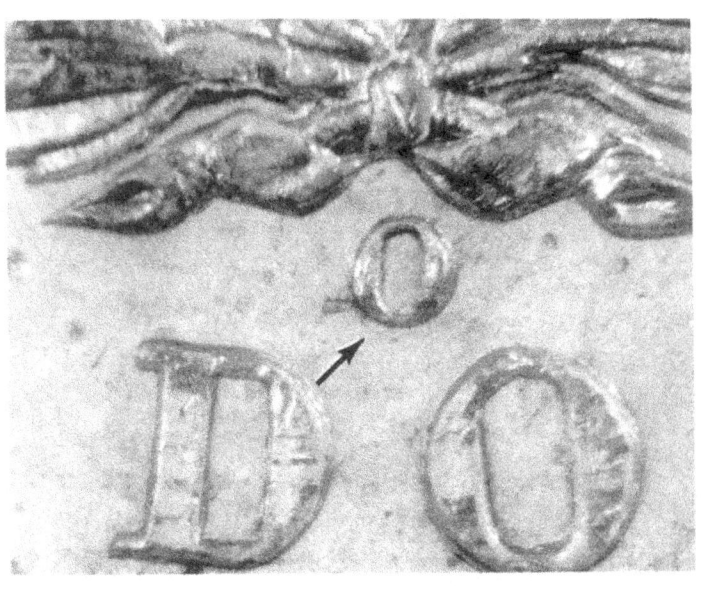

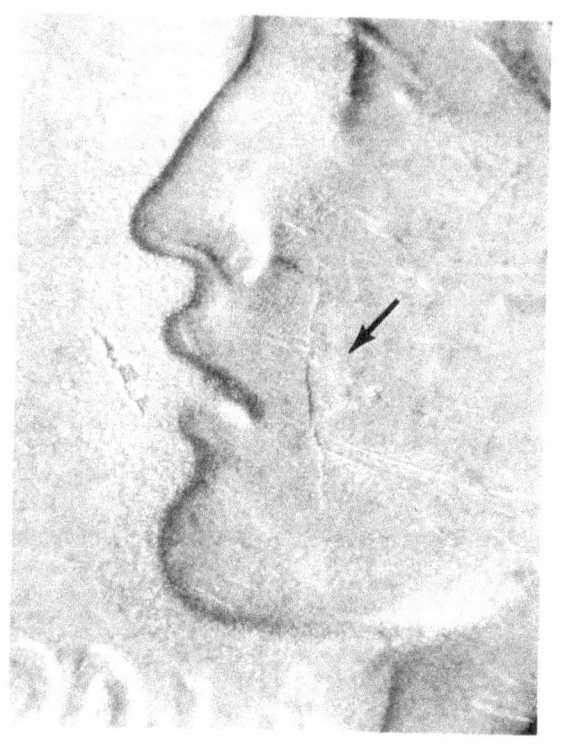

**1922 P
Scar cheek
2 G O   II 1**

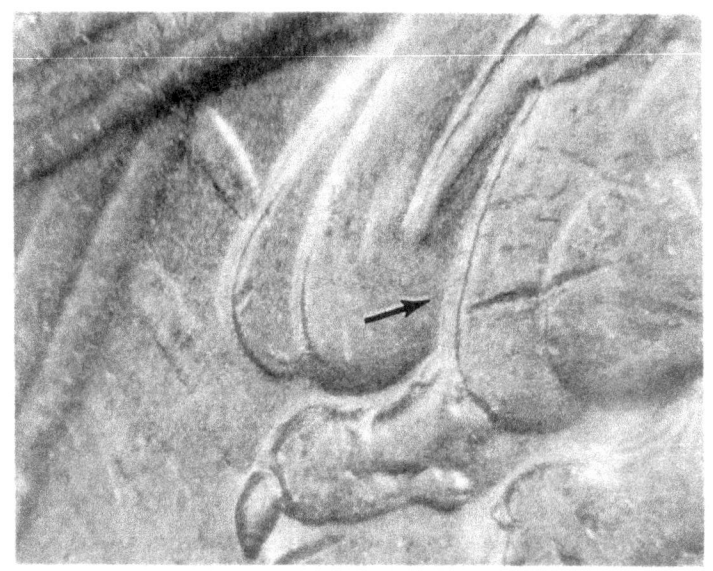

**1922 S
Tripled Reverse
3 R   B^2 b**

1992 VAM BOOK ERRATA LIST

October 24, 1997

Page	VAM #	
85	--	in *Chicago Daily Tribune* letter, insert "at" between "was...once" second line below heading "TEN MORE"
90	–	Morgan April 8 letter, next to last para, last line– change "and" to "than" and "Foreman" to "foreman"
146	14-5	$I^1$10 should be $I^2$10
	14-7	Delete "slightly doubled below...towards rim"
	14-9	3rd line– "data" should be "date"
	14-10	change $I^1$10 to $I^1$5. Delete entire obverse description
152	44	change "blossoms" to "bolls"
154	115	change R-4 to R-6. Add at end of obverse description "Tripled right edges of cotton bolls and leaves."
160	202	change "blossoms" to "bolls"
168	22	II 19 should be II 9
162	6	delete "blossom"
174	56	III 1 should be II 24
202	5	last line– change "the right" to "eagle's left"
204	23	$III^2$17 should be $III^2$36
214	45	reverse description, "carved" should be "curved"
220	16	"doubled" in title should be "tripled". Add after "first 1 doubled"-- "below top and bottom crossbars. First 8 doubled."
	16 O	in photo caption, change "Doubled" to "Tripled"
222	7	C^3c should be C^3e
224	12	C^3i should be C^3j
	23	C^3k should be C^3l
	25	C^3l should be C^3m
	26	Obverse C^3a should be Obverse $III^2$15
227	9 O	photo reversed
228	20	$III^2$20 should be $III^2$4
230	34	$C^3$9 should be C^3g
	38	18-1 should be "and"
239	9 R	O/O Left should be 13 R O/O Lower Left
	10 O	10 O should be 9 O
240	17	"tilted" should be "Tilted" in the title
	15 O	photo title should be 15 R O/O Left
241	16 O	photo title should be 16 R O Tilted Left
	19 O	photo title should be 19 R Over Polished Wing
242	34	title should be "Doubled Date"
251	2	III2 1 should be $III^2$1
	7	$III^2$7 should be $III^2$2
252	3	$III^2$9 should be $III^2$13
254	19	$C^3$1 should be C^3l
255	24 O	24 O should be 24 R
256	38	"Doubled 18-1" should be "Doubled 18-3" in description
259	11	$III^2$12 should be $III^2$11
277	16	$III^2$15 should be $III^2$16
	18	$III^2$16 should be $III^2$17

283	1A R	photo number should be 22 R
284	13	"left" should be "right" end of last line
285	18	III^28 should be III^212
314	11	$C\ ^3g$ should be C^3f
319	–	delete /1892 S at top right
325	5	III O should be IV S
329	7	C^33 should be C^3a
353	3	C^3c should be C^3b
364	22	III^2 should be III^21
388	1	IV should be IV 1
412	–	3RD line "Jones" should be "James"
428	3	B^2c should be B^2b
	4	II 4 should be II 2
429	5	description was left out for 1922 P, add:

5   II 1 • B^2c (Tripled Olive Leaves)   I-3   R-3
  Reverse B^2c– Tripled bottom of olive leaves, back of leg feathers, base of right talon and
  on left rays above tail feathers.

	3	B^2c should be B^2b for 1922 D
430	2	II 4 should be II 2
431	–	1923 D description, first line, insert "it" between "But" and "is"
432	2	B^2i should be B^2b
503	–	3rd para, 7th line, "modem" should be "modern"

FURTHER REFERENCES

Hard Copy Books

Fey, Michael S. 2019. The Top 100 Morgan Dollar Varieties: The VAM Keys. 286 pp. RCI

Fey, Michael S. 2008. *A Decade of Top 100 Insights*. RCI 174 pp.

Van Allen, Leroy. 1991. *RotaFlip Die Rotation Booklet and Guide*. 1991. RCI

Kimpton, M.D., Mark. 2005. *Elite Clashed Morgan Dollars*. RCI 160 pp

Van Allen, Leroy, & A. George Mallis. 2023. *Comprehensive Catalog and Encyclopedia or Morgan & Peace Dollars*. RCI Total 520 pp.

Van Allen, Leroy 2011. *Wonders of Morgan Dollars*. 139 pp. RCI

Van Allen, Leroy 2013. *Wonders of Peace Dollars*. 273 pp. RCI

Van Allen, Leroy 2006. *Morgan Dollars 8 & 7 Over 8 Tail Feather Story*. 52 pp. RCI

Van Allen, Leroy 2010. *1878 P 7 Tail Feather Morgan Dollar Attribution Guide*. 130 pp. RCI

Van Allen, Leroy 2006. *1878 S Morgan Dollar Attribution Guide*. 139 pp. RCI

Van Allen, Leroy 2013. *Die Gouges and Scratches Peace Dollar Attribution Guide. 109 pp* RCI

Van Allen, Leroy 2008. *1921 Scribbles Morgan Dollar Attribution Guide*. 234 pp. RCI

Van Allen, Leroy. 2013. *Misplaced Date Digits Morgan Dollar Attribution Guide*. 57 pp RCI

Van Allen, Leroy. 2017. *Dashed Under 8 Morgan Dollar Attribution Guide*. 53 pp. RCI

Van Allen, Leroy. 2009. *Overdates and Over Mint Marks of Morgan Dollar Attribution Guide*. 53 pp. RCI

Van Allen, Leroy. 2015. *Denticle & Die Impressions Morgan Dollar Attribution Guide*. 109 pp. RCI

Van Allen, Leroy. 2009. *1921 P Infrequently Reeded or Wide Reeding Morgan Dollar Attribution Guide*. 31 pp. RCI

Van Allen, Leroy. 2011 *Amazing Changing 1921 S VAM 1B Thorn Head Morgan Dollar*. 2011. 22 pp. RCI

Van Allen, Leroy. 2009. *1889 P Doubled Ear Morgan Dollar Attribution Guide*. 32 pp. RCI

Van Allen, Leroy. 2016. *Micro o and Other Counterfeit Morgan and Peace Dollars*. 191 pp RCI

Van Allen, Leroy. 2005. *Micro o Mint Mark on Morgan Dollars*. 32 pp. RCI

Van Allen, Leroy. 2005. *Die Markers for 1921 Morgan and Peace Proof Dollars*. 9 pp. RCI

Van Allen, Leroy and Baumgart, John. 1992-Date Various VAM Book Yearly Supplements. RCI

FURTHER REFERENCES

Please check Amazon Kindle for Michael S. Fey, Ph.D., and Leroy Van Allen & A. George Mall is publications. For hard copy print of books, please contact Dr. Fey at RCI, P.O. Box C, Ironia, N J 07845 or eMail: Feyms@aol.com.

Hard copy books are also available at *The Institute for Silver Dollar Education and Research*, at website: *Ilovesilverdollars.org* or by contacting Executive Director John Baumgart at John.Baum gart@comcast.net

Amazon Kindle

Fey, Michael S. 2019. *The Complete Virtual Guide to Pricing Your Morgan Silver Dollars*. 286 pp. RCI

Van Allen, Leroy, & A. George Mallis. 2023. *Part I or II or III of Three. Comprehensive Catalog and Encyclopedia or Morgan & Peace Dollars*. RCI Total 520 pp.

Leroy Van Allen. 2011. *Wonders of Morgan Dollars*. 139 pp. RCI

Leroy Van Allen. 2013. *Wonders of Peace Dollars*. 273 pp. RCI

Leroy Van Allen. 2006. *Morgan Dollars 8 & 7 Over 8 Tail Feather Story*. 52 pp. RCI

Leroy Van Allen. 2010. *1878 P 7 Tail Feather Morgan Dollar Attribution Guide*. 130 pp. RCI

Leroy Van Allen. 2006. *1878 S Morgan Dollar Attribution Guide*. 139 pp. RCI

Fey, Michael S. 2009 The Top 100 Morgan Dollar Varieties: The VAM Keys